180 DAYS™
of
Reading
for First Grade

Name: _____   Date: _____

Unit 4
WEEK 3
DAY
4–5

As You Read Underline something that is fun or interesting. Share it with a friend or adult.

Ski School

Zoe and Taj take skiing lessons the first day. First, they learn how to get up after a fall. They fall down a lot. But it is still fun. That afternoon, they ride the ski lift to the top of a small hill. Soon they can zip down hill without falling. They are skiers!

135043—180 Days of Reading   27

Authors
Stephanie Kraus
Carol Huey-Gatewood, M.A.Ed.

Program Credits

Corinne Burton, M.A.Ed., *President and Publisher*
Emily R. Smith, M.A.Ed., *SVP of Content Development*
Véronique Bos, *Vice President of Creative*
Lynette Ordoñez, *Content Manager*
Melissa Laughlin, *Editor*
Ashley Oberhaus, M.Ed., *Content Specialist*
David Slayton, *Assistant Editor*
Jill Malcolm, *Graphic Designer*

Image Credits: p.85 Shutterstock/Wangkun Jia; p.131 Shutterstock/Marcella Miriello; p.157 Shutterstock/Proshkin Aleksandr; p.158 Shutterstock/Chad Robertson Media; p.167 Shutterstock/sophiecat; all other images from Shutterstock and/or iStock

Standards

© Copyright 2010 National Governors Association Center for Best Practices and Council of Chief State School Officers. All rights reserved.
© Copyright 2007–2023 Texas Education Agency (TEA). All Rights Reserved.
© 2023 TESOL International Association
© 2023 Board of Regents of the University of Wisconsin System

A division of Teacher Created Materials
5482 Argosy Avenue
Huntington Beach, CA 92649
www.tcmpub.com/shell-education
ISBN 979-8-7659-1803-6
© 2024 Shell Educational Publishing, Inc.
Printed in China 51497

Table of Contents

Introduction

The Need for Practice

To be successful in today's reading classroom, students must deeply understand both concepts and procedures so that they can discuss and demonstrate their understanding. Demonstrating understanding is a process that must be continually practiced for students to be successful. According to Robert Marzano, "Practice has always been, and always will be, a necessary ingredient to learning procedural knowledge at a level at which students execute it independently" (2010, 83). Practice is especially important to help students apply reading comprehension strategies and word-study skills. *180 Days of Reading* offers teachers and parents a full page of reading comprehension and word recognition practice activities for each day of the school year.

The Science of Reading

For some people, reading comes easily. They barely remember how it happened. For others, learning to read takes more effort.

The goal of reading research is to understand the differences in how people learn to read and find the best ways to help all students learn. The term *Science of Reading* is commonly used to refer to this body of research. It helps people understand how to provide instruction in learning the code of the English language, how to develop fluency, and how to navigate challenging text and make sense of it.

Much of this research has been around for decades. In fact, in the late 1990s, Congress commissioned a review of the reading research. In 2000, the National Reading Panel (NRP) published a report that became the backbone of the Science of Reading. The NRP report highlights five components of effective reading instruction. These include the following:

- **Phonemic Awareness:** understanding and manipulating individual speech sounds
- **Phonics:** matching sounds to letters for use in reading and spelling
- **Fluency:** reading connected text accurately and smoothly
- **Vocabulary:** knowing the meanings of words in speech and in print
- **Reading Comprehension:** understanding what is read

There are two commonly referenced frameworks that build on reading research and provide a visual way for people to understand what is needed to learn to read. In the mid-1980s, a framework called the Simple View of Reading was introduced (Gough and Tunmer 1986). It shows that reading comprehension is possible when students are able to decode (or read) the words and have the language to understand the words.

The Simple View of Reading

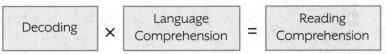

Decoding × Language Comprehension = Reading Comprehension

Another framework that builds on the research behind the Science of Reading is Scarborough's Reading Rope (Scarborough 2001). It shows specific skills needed for both language comprehension and word recognition. The "strands" of the rope for language comprehension include having background content knowledge, knowing vocabulary, understanding language structure, having verbal reasoning, and understanding literacy. Word recognition includes phonological awareness, decoding skills, and sight recognition of familiar words (Scarborough 2001). As individual skills are strengthened and practiced, they become increasingly strategic and automatic to promote reading comprehension.

The Science of Reading (cont.)

Many parts of our understanding of how people learn to read stand the test of time and have been confirmed by more recent studies. However, new research continues to add to the understanding of reading. Some of this research shows the importance of wide reading (reading about a variety of topics), motivation, and self-regulation. The conversation will never be over, as new research will continue to refine the understanding of how people learn to read. There is always more to learn!

180 Days of Reading has been informed by this reading research. This series provides opportunities for students to practice the skills that years of research indicate contribute to reading growth. There are several features in this book that are supported by the Science of Reading.

Text Selection

- Carefully chosen texts offer experiences in a **wide range of text types**. Each unit includes nonfiction, fiction, and a nontraditional text type or genre (e.g., letters, newspaper articles, advertisements, menus).

- Texts intentionally build upon one another to help students **build background knowledge** from day to day.

- Engaging with texts on the same topic for a thematic unit enables students to become familiar with related **vocabulary**, **language structure**, and **literacy knowledge**. This allows reading to become increasingly strategic and automatic, leading to better **fluency** and **comprehension**.

Activity Design

- Specific **language comprehension** and **word-recognition skills** are reinforced throughout the activities.

- Each text includes a purpose for reading and an opportunity to practice various reading strategies through annotation. This promotes **close reading** of the text.

- Paired fiction and nonfiction texts are used to promote **comparison** and encourage students to **make connections** between texts within a unit.

- Students **write to demonstrate understanding** of the texts. Students provide written responses in a variety of forms, including short answers, open-ended responses, and creating their own versions of nontraditional texts.

This book provides the regular practice of reading skills that students need as they develop into excellent readers.

How to Use This Resource

Unit Structure Overview

This resource is organized into twelve units. Each three-week unit follows a consistent format for ease of use.

Week 1: Nonfiction

Day 1	Students read nonfiction and answer multiple-choice questions.
Day 2	Students read nonfiction and answer multiple-choice questions.
Day 3	Students read nonfiction and answer multiple-choice, short-answer, and open-response questions.
Day 4	Students read a longer nonfictional text, answer multiple-choice questions, and complete graphic organizers.
Day 5	Students reread the text from Day 4 and answer reading-response questions.

Week 2: Fiction

Day 1	Students read fiction and answer multiple-choice questions.
Day 2	Students read fiction and answer multiple-choice questions.
Day 3	Students read fiction and answer multiple-choice, short-answer, and open-response questions.
Day 4	Students read a longer fictional text, answer multiple-choice questions, and complete graphic organizers.
Day 5	Students reread the text from Day 4 and answer reading-response questions.

Week 3: Nontraditional Text

Day 1	Students read nontraditional text and answer multiple-choice and open-response questions.
Day 2	Students complete close-reading activities with paired texts from the unit.
Day 3	Students complete close-reading activities with paired texts from the unit.
Day 4	Students create their own nontraditional texts.
Day 5	Students write their own versions of the nontraditional text from Day 1.

How to Use This Resource (cont.)

Unit Structure Overview (cont.)

Paired Texts

State standards have brought into focus the importance of preparing students for college and career success by expanding their critical-thinking and analytical skills. It is no longer enough for students to read and comprehend a single text on a topic. Rather, the integration of ideas across texts is crucial for a more comprehensive understanding of themes presented by authors.

Literacy specialist Jennifer Soalt has written that paired texts are "uniquely suited to scaffolding and extending students' comprehension" (2005, 680). She identifies three ways in which paired fiction and nonfiction are particularly effective in increasing comprehension: the building of background knowledge, the development of vocabulary, and the increase in student motivation (Soalt 2005).

Each three-week unit in *180 Days of Reading* is connected by a common theme or topic. Packets of each week's or each unit's practice pages can be prepared for students.

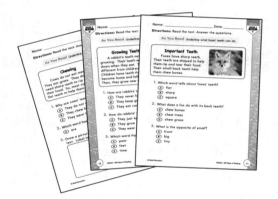

During Week 1, students read nonfictional texts and answer questions.

During Week 2, students read fictional texts and answer questions.

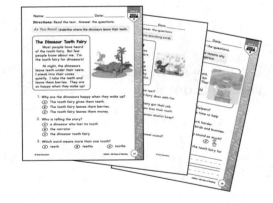

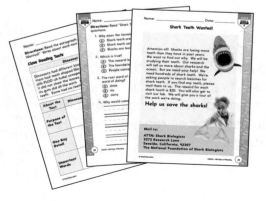

During Week 3, students read nontraditional texts (advertisements, poems, letters, etc.), answer questions, and complete close-reading and writing activities.

How to Use This Resource *(cont.)*

Student Practice Pages

Practice pages reinforce grade-level skills across a variety of reading concepts for each day of the school year. Each day's reading activity is provided as a full practice page, making them easy to prepare and implement as part of a morning routine, at the beginning of each reading lesson, or as homework.

Practice Pages for Weeks 1 and 2

Days 1 and 2 of each week follow a consistent format, with a short text passage and multiple-choice questions.

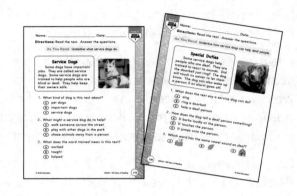

Days 3 and 4 have a combination of multiple-choice, short-answer, and open-response questions.

On day 5, students complete text-based writing prompts.

As You Read Underline something that is new or interesting. Share it with a friend or adult.

The As You Read activities give students a purpose for reading the texts and provide opportunities to practice various reading skills and strategies.

How to Use This Resource *(cont.)*

Student Practice Pages *(cont.)*

Practice Pages for Week 3

Day 1 of this week follows a consistent format, with a nontraditional text and multiple-choice and open-response questions.

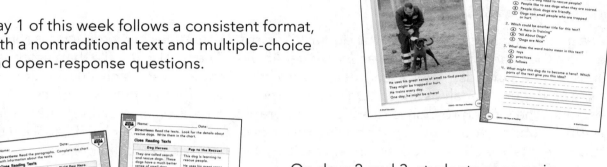

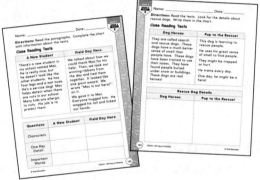

On days 2 and 3, students engage in close-reading activities of paired texts. Students are encouraged to compare and contrast different aspects of the texts they read throughout the unit.

On days 4 and 5, students think about the texts in the unit, respond to a writing prompt, and construct their own versions of diverse texts. Students are encouraged to use information from texts throughout the unit to inspire and support their writing.

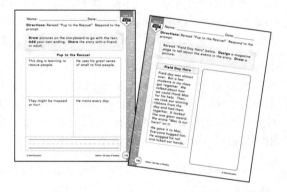

Instructional Options

180 Days of Reading is a flexible resource that can be used in various instructional settings for different purposes.

- Use these student pages as daily warm-up activities or as review.

- Work with students in small groups, allowing them to focus on specific skills. This setting also lends itself to partner and group discussions about the texts.

- Student pages in this resource can be completed independently during center times and as activities for early finishers.

How to Use This Resource (cont.)

Diagnostic Assessment

The practice pages in this book can be used as diagnostic assessments. These activity pages require students to think critically, respond to text-dependent questions, and utilize reading and writing skills and strategies. (An answer key for the practice pages is provided starting on page 230.)

For each unit, analysis sheets are provided as *Microsoft Word®* files in the digital resources. There is a *Class Analysis Sheet* and an *Individual Analysis Sheet*. Use the file that matches your assessment needs. After each week, record how many answers each student got correct on the unit's analysis sheet. Only record the answers for the multiple-choice questions. The written-response questions and graphic organizers can be evaluated using the writing rubric or other evaluation tools (see below). At the end of each unit, analyze the data on the analysis sheet to determine instructional focuses for your child or class.

The diagnostic analysis tools included in the digital resources allow for quick evaluation and ongoing monitoring of student work. See at a glance which reading genre students may need to focus on further to develop proficiency.

Using the Results to Differentiate Instruction

Once results are gathered and analyzed, use the data to inform the way to differentiate instruction. The data can help determine which concepts are the most difficult for students and that need additional instructional support and continued practice.

The results of the diagnostic analysis may show that an entire class is struggling with a particular genre. If these concepts have been taught in the past, this indicates that further instruction or reteaching is necessary. If these concepts have not been taught yet, this data is a great preassessment and demonstrates that students do not have a working knowledge of the concepts.

The results of the diagnostic analysis may also show that an individual or small group of students is struggling with a particular concept or group of concepts. Consider pulling aside these students while others are working independently to instruct further on the concept(s). You can also use the results to help identify individuals or groups of proficient students who are ready for enrichment or above-grade-level instruction. These students may benefit from independent learning contracts or more challenging activities.

Writing Rubric

A rubric for written responses is provided on page 229. Display the rubric for students to reference as they write. Score students' written responses, and provide them with feedback on their writing.

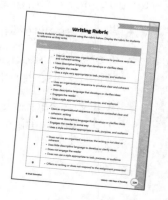

Name: _____ Date: _____

Directions: Read the text. Answer the questions.

As You Read Underline what foxes' teeth can do.

Important Teeth

Foxes have sharp teeth. Their teeth are shaped to help them rip and tear their food. Their small back teeth help them chew bones.

1. Which word tells about foxes' teeth?
   - (A) flat
   - (B) sharp
   - (C) square

2. What does a fox do with its back teeth?
   - (A) chew bones
   - (B) chew trees
   - (C) chew grass

3. What is the opposite of *small*?
   - (A) front
   - (B) big
   - (C) tiny

Name: _____ Date: _____

Directions: Read the text. Answer the questions.

As You Read > Underline the facts about children's teeth.

Growing Teeth

A rabbit's teeth never stop growing. Their teeth wear down when they eat. This is different from children's teeth. Children have teeth that become loose and fall out. Then, they grow new teeth.

1. How are rabbits' teeth different from your teeth?
   - (A) They never fall out.
   - (B) They keep growing.
   - (C) They eat carrots.

2. How do rabbits' teeth wear down?
   - (A) They just keep growing.
   - (B) They grow in crooked.
   - (C) They wear down when rabbits eat.

3. Which word rhymes with *eat*?
   - (A) pear
   - (B) feet
   - (C) time

Directions: Read the text. Answer the questions.

As You Read ⟩ Underline a fact that is new to you.

Chewing

Cows do not eat meat. They eat grass. They do not need sharp teeth to rip and tear their food. So, most cows have flat teeth to help them chew.

1. Why are cows' teeth not sharp?

   Ⓐ They do not need to tear meat.

   Ⓑ They chew bones and grass.

   Ⓒ They wear them down by chewing grass.

2. Which word has the same vowel sound as *feet*?

   Ⓐ are   Ⓑ tear   Ⓒ meat

3. Draw a picture that shows the main idea of this text. Label important parts of the picture.

Name: _____ Date: _____

As You Read Underline something that is new or interesting. Share it with a friend or adult.

Dinosaur Teeth

Dinosaurs had different kinds of teeth. Some of them had teeth shaped like spoons. The diplodocus (dih-PLOD-uh-kuhs) scooped leaves from trees. But it did not chew the leaves. It swallowed them. Then, its guts did all the work. Some dinosaurs had pointed teeth. Some had no teeth at all!

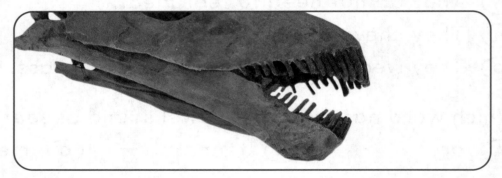

diplodocus teeth

T-rex teeth

Directions: Read "Dinosaur Teeth." Answer the questions.

1. What is the main idea?

(A) Dinosaurs eat grass and leaves.

(B) You should take care of your teeth.

(C) You can learn about dinosaurs from looking at their teeth.

2. What did dinosaurs with sharp teeth likely eat?

(A) meat and other dinosaurs

(B) soft food like fruit

(C) trees and bushes

3. Which dinosaur did **not** chew?

(A) T-rex

(B) all dinosaurs

(C) diplodocus

4. Write three details from the text about dinosaur teeth.

1.	
2.	
3.	

Name: _____ Date: _____

Directions: Reread "Dinosaur Teeth." Respond to the prompt.

> **Think** about what you learned about dinosaur teeth. Imagine a new kind of dinosaur. What would it look like? What kind of teeth would it have? What would it eat? **Write** about the dinosaur. **Draw** a picture.

_____

_____

_____

_____

_____

_____

_____

_____

Directions: Read the text. Answer the questions.

As You Read > Underline where the dinosaurs leave their teeth.

The Dinosaur Tooth Fairy

Most people have heard of the tooth fairy. But few people know about me. I'm the tooth fairy for dinosaurs!

At night, the dinosaurs leave teeth under their nests. I sneak into their caves quietly. I take the teeth and leave them berries. They are so happy when they wake up!

1. Why are the dinosaurs happy when they wake up?
   - (A) The tooth fairy gives them teeth.
   - (B) The tooth fairy leaves them berries.
   - (C) The tooth fairy leaves them money.

2. Who is telling the story?
   - (A) a dinosaur who lost its tooth
   - (B) a dentist
   - (C) the dinosaur tooth fairy

3. Which word means more than one tooth?
   - (A) teeth   (C) tooths
   - (B) teeths

Name: _____ Date: _____

Directions: Read the text. Answer the questions.

As You Read ⟩ Underline describing words.

The Dinosaur Dentist

I work as a tooth fairy. I see all kinds of teeth. Some teeth are big, and some teeth are small. Some teeth are sharp, and some teeth are dull. I bring everything to the dinosaur dentist. He keeps some of the teeth that are healthy. He gives them to the dinosaurs who need them.

1. Which sentence summarizes the text?

   Ⓐ It explains what the tooth fairy and dentist do with the teeth.

   Ⓑ It explains how the tooth fairy got their job.

   Ⓒ It explains why the dinosaurs lose their teeth.

2. What kind of teeth does the dinosaur dentist keep?

   Ⓐ the ones that are healthy

   Ⓑ all of the sharp ones

   Ⓒ the ones in the bag

3. Which two words have the same vowel sound?

   Ⓐ *put* and *dull*

   Ⓑ *teeth* and *need*

   Ⓒ *night* and *gives*

Name: _____ Date: _____

Directions: Read the text. Answer the questions.

As You Read > Underline reasons why the tooth fairy's job is dangerous.

Tooth Fairy Troubles

Being a tooth fairy is hard work. My job is dangerous. I could get bit or eaten! I think I need helpers. That would give me time to help other animals besides dinosaurs. I would love to work with cows or bunnies. They are less scary!

1. Why does the tooth fairy want helpers?

Ⓐ The tooth fairy wants more time to help other animals.

Ⓑ The tooth fairy needs to work harder.

Ⓒ The tooth fairy is afraid of bunnies.

2. Which word has the same ending sound as *much*?

Ⓐ   Ⓑ   Ⓒ

3. Would it be less scary to be the tooth fairy for bunnies? Why?

_____

- -

_____

- -

_____

Name: _____ Date: _____

Dear Tooth Fairy

I get so many letters from the dinosaurs! I don't know how they got my address. They write to me and ask for more berries in return for their teeth. At least, I think that's what they want. Their handwriting is not very good.

I don't have time to write them back. I wish they would be happy with what they get! I wonder how they got so spoiled.

These letters are starting to make me feel annoyed with my work. I think I need a new job. Someone out there might need to hire a fairy. I really hope so. I will have to spread the word.

Fairy
for Hire

Name: _____ Date: _____

Directions: Read "Dear Tooth Fairy." Answer the questions.

1. What is one thing the tooth fairy is complaining about?

   Ⓐ The dinosaurs aren't losing as many teeth.

   Ⓑ The dinosaurs want more berries for their teeth.

   Ⓒ The dinosaurs are happy with what they get.

2. Which sentence is **not** true?

   Ⓐ The tooth fairy gets many letters from dinosaurs.

   Ⓑ The dinosaurs are spoiled.

   Ⓒ The tooth fairy writes back to all the dinosaurs.

3. What does the phrase *spread the word* mean in this text?

   Ⓐ Don't tell anyone.

   Ⓑ Let people know.

   Ⓒ Only tell one person.

4. Trace the words in the center oval. Write words in the ovals that describe the tooth fairy's problems.

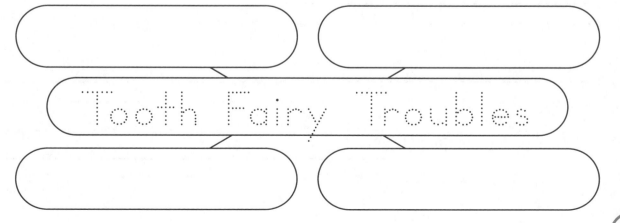

Tooth Fairy Troubles

Name: _____ Date: _____

Directions: Reread "Dear Tooth Fairy." Respond to the prompt.

Imagine the tooth fairy finds a new job. They find a help wanted ad for pizza delivery. **Write** a letter from the tooth fairy to the pizza place. Have the tooth fairy tell why they want the job. Give one reason why the fairy will be good at the job. **Draw** a picture.

Shark Teeth Wanted!

Attention all! Sharks are losing more teeth than they have in past years. We want to find out why. We will be studying their teeth. Our research will tell us more about sharks and the ocean. But we need your help! We need hundreds of shark teeth. We're asking people to search beaches for shark teeth. If you find any teeth, please mail them to us. The reward for each shark tooth is $20. You will also get to visit our lab. We will give you a tour of the work we're doing.

Help us save the sharks!

Mail to:

ATTN: Shark Biologists
The National Foundation of Shark Biologists
3273 Research Lane
Seaside, California, 92307

Name: _____ Date: _____

Directions: Read "Shark Teeth Wanted." Answer the questions.

1. Why does the foundation want shark teeth?
   - (A) Shark teeth are dangerous.
   - (B) Shark teeth can be made into necklaces.
   - (C) Sharks are losing more teeth than in the past.

2. Which is true?
   - (A) The reward for each shark tooth is $20.
   - (B) The foundation is in Sacramento, California.
   - (C) People cannot visit the research lab.

3. The root word of *studying* is *study*. What is the root word of *doing*?
   - (A) does
   - (B) do
   - (C) done

4. Why do you think someone would want to find shark teeth?

   _____

   _____

   _____

   _____

   _____

   _____

Name: _____ Date: _____

Directions: Read the text. Study "Shark Teeth Wanted!"
Write about each text on the chart.

Close-Reading Text

Dinosaur Teeth
Dinosaurs had different kinds of teeth. Some of them had teeth shaped like spoons. The diplodocus (dih-PLOD-uh-kuhs) scooped leaves from trees. But it did not chew the leaves. It swallowed them. Then, its guts did all the work. Some dinosaurs had pointed teeth. Some had no teeth at all!

About the Text	Dinosaur Teeth	Shark Teeth Wanted
Purpose of the Text		
One Key Detail		
Important Words		

Name: _____ Date: _____

Directions: Read the texts. Look for what the tooth fairy says about their job. Write them in the chart.

Close-Reading Texts

The Dinosaur Dentist	Tooth Fairy Troubles
I work as a tooth fairy. I see all kinds of teeth. Some teeth are big, and some teeth are small. Some teeth are sharp, and some teeth are dull. I bring everything to the dinosaur dentist.	Being a tooth fairy is hard work. My job is dangerous. I could get bit or eaten! I think I need helpers.

The Dinosaur Dentist	Tooth Fairy Troubles

Name: _____ Date: _____

Directions: Think about the texts from this unit. Respond to the prompt.

Imagine you are the dinosaur tooth fairy. **Draw** what the fairy might dream about. **Write** about the dream.

_____

- -

_____

- -

_____

- -

_____

- -

_____

Name: _____ Date: _____

Directions: Reread "Shark Teeth Wanted." Respond to the prompt.

You have found some shark teeth. You are sending them to the shark biologists. **Write** a letter telling them about the shark teeth you are sending. Ask them some questions. **Draw** the shark teeth.

_____

- - - - - - - - - - - - - - -

_____ ,

_____

- - - - - - - - - - - - - - - - -

_____

_____

- - - - - - - - - - - - - - - - -

_____

_____

- - - - - - - - - - - - - - -

_____

Name: _____ Date: _____

Directions: Read the text. Answer the questions.

As You Read › Underline the season in the text.

Hungry Bears

Black bears eat all summer long. They love fruits, nuts, and roots. They can gain 30 pounds in one week. That is a lot!

1. Which sentence is true?

Ⓐ Black bears get thinner in summer.

Ⓑ Black bears eat less in summer.

Ⓒ Black bears get fatter in summer.

2. What do black bears like to eat?

Ⓐ hay and grass

Ⓑ nuts and fruit

Ⓒ trees and bushes

3. The word *summer* has two syllables: *sum–mer*. Which word has two syllables?

Ⓐ better

Ⓑ asked

Ⓒ where

Name: _____ Date: _____

Directions: Read the text. Answer the questions.

As You Read > Underline facts you think are interesting.

Bear Homes

Black bears make dens in the fall. They may find caves or holes in trees. They gather leaves and twigs to make beds. Some black bears use leaves and twigs to make nests on the ground.

1. What do black bears do in the fall?
   - (A) find a place to eat
   - (B) find a place for a den
   - (C) find a place for food

2. What do bears use to make dens?
   - (A) leaves and twigs
   - (B) feathers
   - (C) caves and trees

3. Which word rhymes with *nest*?
   - (A)
   - (B)
   - (C)

Directions: Read the text. Answer the questions.

A Place to Rest

Black bears go into their dens when winter starts. They curl up into balls. Their heads and paws stay warm while they sleep.

1. Why do bears curl up into balls?
   - (A) to help them stay warm
   - (B) to help them stay awake
   - (C) to help them eat

2. Which word has the same vowel sound as *den*?

   (A)   (B)   (C)

3. Where do you feel warm and safe like a bear in a den?

   _____

   _____

   _____

Name: _____ Date: _____

A Very Long Nap

You may sleep for 10 hours at a time. Black bears can sleep for 100 days at a time! Their bodies slow down while they hibernate in the winter. Their bodies use up all the fat they stored from the food they ate in summer.

Bears wake up in the spring. They are much thinner. It is time for them to eat a big breakfast!

Directions: Read "A Very Long Nap." Answer the questions.

1. Why are bears thinner in spring?
   - Ⓐ They have used up their body fat.
   - Ⓑ They have been running a lot.
   - Ⓒ They have eaten fruit and roots.

2. What do bears do when they hibernate?
   - Ⓐ eat
   - Ⓑ sleep
   - Ⓒ talk

3. How are you like a black bear?
   - Ⓐ We both have paws.
   - Ⓑ We both sleep all winter.
   - Ⓒ We both eat and sleep.

4. Trace the topic of the text. Write two facts about bear hibernation.

Bear Hibernation

Name: _____ Date: _____

Directions: Reread "A Very Long Nap." Respond to the prompt.

Think about how bears hibernate. Imagine you are a bear. What would it feel like to wake up? **Write** what you think a bear feels like when it wakes up in the spring. **Draw** a picture.

_____

- -

_____

- -

_____

- -

_____

- -

_____

135043—180 Days of Reading   © Shell Education

Directions: Read the text. Answer the questions.

> **As You Read** Underline the type of animal that is missing.

A Missing Pet

Kim says, "Mom, can you help me find my turtle? He is missing. I have looked everywhere for him."

1. Who is Kim talking to?
   - (A) her turtle
   - (B) her dad
   - (C) her mom

2. What is Kim's problem?
   - (A) She needs to feed her turtle.
   - (B) Her turtle is missing.
   - (C) Mom needs to help Kim.

3. What is another word for *looked*?
   - (A) find
   - (B) gone
   - (C) searched

Name: _____ **Date:** _____

Directions: Read the text. Answer the questions.

As You Read > Underline Mom's idea.

Mom Has an Idea

Mom says, "I think Tork is hiding."

"Why?" asks Kim.

"Winter is coming. Box turtles sleep a lot in winter," Mom says.

1. What is the name of the turtle?
   - (A) Kim
   - (B) Tork
   - (C) Box

2. Why is the turtle hiding?
   - (A) to find a place to sleep
   - (B) to find food
   - (C) to find another turtle

3. The word *hiding* comes from *hide*. What word does *riding* come from?
   - (A) rid
   - (B) ride
   - (C) ding

Name: _____ Date: _____

Directions: Read the text. Answer the questions.

As You Read ⟩ Underline the turtle's name.

A Sleepy Turtle

Kim asks, "Why does Tork want to sleep?"

"Turtles slow down in winter," Mom says. "They sleep all winter, just like bears do. We should look for Tork in quiet and cool places."

1. Which animals slow down in the winter?

(A) turtles

(B) rabbits

(C) dogs

2. What is the opposite of *slow*?

(A) low

(B) funny

(C) fast

2. How are turtles and bears alike?

_____

_ _ _ _ _ _ _ _ _ _ _ _ _ _ _ _ _

_____

_ _ _ _ _ _ _ _ _ _ _ _ _ _ _ _ _

_____

Name: _____ Date: _____

Finding Tork

Kim and Mom find Tork in the closet.

Kim asks, "When will he wake up?"

Mom says, "Tork will wake up when he gets hungry."

Kim checks on Tork to be sure he is okay as he sleeps all winter. One day, she can't find him in the closet. Kim checks each room. Then, she finds Tork right next to his tank. He is ready to eat!

Name: _____ Date: _____

Directions: Read "Finding Tork." Answer the questions.

1. Why does Kim check on Tork?

(A) She wants to give him water.

(B) She wants to be sure he is okay.

(C) She wants to put him in his tank.

2. How do you think Kim feels when she finds Tork?

(A) thankful

(B) upset

(C) tired

3. What has Kim learned?

(A) Turtles can sleep for months.

(B) Turtles like winter.

(C) Turtles make bad pets.

4. Write the number 1, 2, or 3 next to each sentence to retell the story in the correct order.

	Then, she finds Tork right next to his tank.
	Kim and Mom find Tork in the closet.
	Kim checks on Tork as he sleeps all winter.

Name: _____ Date: _____

Directions: Reread "Finding Tork." Respond to the prompt.

Think about all the places that turtles can sleep. How do they find the right place? **Write** about a turtle that is looking for a place to sleep all winter. **Draw** a picture.

_____
_ _
_____
_____
_ _
_____
_____
_____
_ _
_____
_ _
_____

Name: _____ Date: _____

Hibernation Sign

Shh, I'm Hibernating!

Please be quiet! I'm a groundhog. I found the perfect spot to hibernate this winter. It's under this shed you see here. I searched for weeks! I've made a cozy little home down here. I have eaten lots of food to get me through. Don't you dare think about taking my spot!

Name: _____ Date: _____

Directions: Read "Hibernation Sign." Answer the questions.

1. Why doesn't the groundhog want to be disturbed?
   - (A) It is scared.
   - (B) It is eating.
   - (C) It is hibernating.

2. When does this text take place?
   - (A) summer
   - (B) winter
   - (C) July

3. What does the word *cozy* mean?
   - (A) cold
   - (B) comfortable
   - (C) little

4. What is the main idea of this text?

   _____

   _____

   _____

   _____

   _____

   _____

   _____

Name: _____ Date: _____

Directions: Read these texts. Look for words or phrases about hibernation. Underline them. Write two from each text in the chart.

Close-Reading Texts

A Very Long Nap	Hibernation Sign
Black bears can sleep for 100 days at a time! Their bodies slow down while they hibernate in the winter. Their bodies use up all the fat they stored from the food they ate in summer. Bears wake up in the spring.	Please be quiet! I'm a groundhog. I found the perfect spot to hibernate this winter. It's under this shed you see here. I searched for weeks! I've made a cozy little home down here. I have eaten lots of food to get me through.

Text	Hibernation Words/Phrases
A Very Long Nap	1. _____ 2. _____
Hibernation Sign	1. _____ 2. _____

Name: _____ Date: _____

Directions: Read these texts. Write one way they are similar. Write one way they are different.

Close-Reading Texts

A Sleepy Turtle	Kim asks, "Why does Tork want to sleep?" "Turtles slow down in winter," Mom says. "They sleep all winter, just like bears do. We should look for Tork in quiet and cool places."
A Place to Rest	Black bears go into their dens when winter starts. They curl up into balls. Their heads and paws stay warm while they sleep.

Similar	_____ ------------------------------- _____ ------------------------------- _____
Different	_____ ------------------------------- _____ ------------------------------- _____

Name: _____ Date: _____

Directions: Think about the texts from this unit. Respond to the prompt.

Write six words about hibernation in the word bank. Trace the word *Hibernation*. Write the words on the lines to make a poem. Draw an animal hibernating in a den.

Word Bank

Hibernation

Name: _____ Date: _____

Directions: Reread "Hibernation Sign" and "Finding Tork." Respond to the prompt.

Think about Tork the turtle. **Write** about hibernating from Tork's point of view. Tell about where Tork is and how he feels. **Draw** Tork in the closet. Draw a "Do Not Disturb" sign for Tork.

_____

_____

_____

_____

_____

_____

_____

Name: _____ Date: _____

Directions: Read the text. Answer the questions.

As You Read ⟩ Circle the season in the text.

Fun in the Snow

One winter day, Sherman Poppen saw his daughter stand on her sled. She rode it down the hill. It looked like a lot of fun to him.

1. What did Sherman Poppen see?

   (A) his daughter lying flat while riding her sled

   (B) his daughter sitting while riding her sled

   (C) his daughter standing while riding her sled

2. What did Sherman Poppen think about his daughter on her sled?

   (A) She could fall off.

   (B) It must be fun.

   (C) She should sit down.

3. Which picture shows a word that sounds just like *rode*?

   (A)   (B)   (C)

Name: _____ Date: _____

Directions: Read the text. Answer the questions.

As You Read ▷ Underline what Mr. Poppen did.

Mr. Poppen's Idea

Mr. Poppen had an idea. He got two skis. He nailed wood on top to keep them together. The skis made a board. His daughter stood on it and rode it down the hill.

1. What did Mr. Poppen use to make his idea?
   (A) a sled
   (B) two boards
   (C) two skis

2. What did he make?
   (A) something to sit on
   (B) something to stand on
   (C) something to lie on

3. What does the word *idea* mean?
   (A) a ski
   (B) a trick
   (C) a thought

Name: _____ Date: _____

Directions: Read the text. Answer the questions.

As You Read ▷ Underline what Mr. Poppen added to the skis.

Making it Better

Mr. Poppen added a rope to the front of the skis. Now it could be controlled. It was even more fun to ride. Now all the children wanted one!

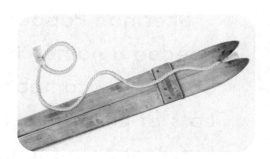

1. Why did all the children want one?

  Ⓐ There was snow outside.

  Ⓑ It looked like fun to ride.

  Ⓒ His daughter liked to share.

2. What does *added* mean?

  Ⓐ used

  Ⓑ made

  Ⓒ put on

3. How did Mr. Poppen make his idea better?

_____

_ _ _ _ _ _ _ _ _ _ _ _ _ _ _ _ _ _ _

_____

_____

_ _ _ _ _ _ _ _ _ _ _ _ _ _ _ _ _ _ _

_____

Name: _____   Date: _____

As You Read > Underline something that is new or interesting. Share it with a friend or adult.

The Snurfer

Sherman Poppen had made a great toy. It needed a name. His wife called it a snurfer. Soon a toy company started making them. Lots of children used them for a few years. Later, people thought of ways to make them better. You may have used what came next: the snowboard!

Directions: Read "The Snurfer." Answer the questions.

1. Which words do you think the word *snurfer* came from?

   Ⓐ snow and surfer

   Ⓑ sled and skis

   Ⓒ sled and surf

2. Why did people make changes to the snurfer?

   Ⓐ so it would work even better

   Ⓑ so it would be even smaller

   Ⓒ so it could be painted

3. What is the main idea?

   Ⓐ Mrs. Poppen gave the name *snurfer* to a toy.

   Ⓑ A toy company made snurfers.

   Ⓒ The snowboard began with a toy called a *snurfer*.

4. Write the words *first*, *then*, or *last* next to the sentences to retell the story in the correct order.

	People thought of ways to make the snurfer better.
	A toy company made the snurfer and children used them.
	Sherman's wife called the toy a *snurfer*.

Name: _____ Date: _____

Directions: Reread "The Snurfer." Respond to the prompt.

Think about Mr. Poppens' idea. He put two sports together. But what if he put skiing with another sport? **Write** about what new toy could be made. **Draw** a picture.

_____

- -

_____

- -

_____

- -

_____

- -

_____

- -

Directions: Read the text. Answer the questions.

As You Read ⟩ Underline what Zoe and Taj pack.

Getting Ready

Zoe and Taj get ready for a trip. They pack sweaters and warm pants. They put on jackets, hats, scarves, and gloves.

1. Who is getting ready for a trip?
   - (A) sweaters and pants
   - (B) Zoe and Taj
   - (C) jackets and hats

2. Which sentence is true?
   - (A) They are going somewhere cold.
   - (B) They are going somewhere hot.
   - (C) They are going to a beach.

3. Which word is spelled correctly?
   - (A) rede
   - (B) reade
   - (C) ready

Name: _____ Date: _____

Directions: Read the text. Answer the questions.

As You Read ⟩ Underline what the weather is like.

The Trip

Zoe and Taj are ready for a long drive in the car. It snows hard in the mountains. Dad stops to get hot chocolate.

---

1. Why do you think they will have a long drive?

    (A) They are going a long way.

    (B) They are going to sleep in the car.

    (C) They are going home soon.

2. Where is it snowing?

    (A) at their house

    (B) in the mountains

    (C) in the city

3. The word *chocolate* has 3 syllables: *choc-o-late*. Which word also has three syllables?

    (A) ready

    (B) something

    (C) beautiful

Name: _____ Date: _____

Unit 3
WEEK 2
DAY
3

Directions: Read the text. Answer the questions.

As You Read Underline what the girls do in the morning.

Time for School

The family gets to their hotel long after dark. The next morning, Zoe and Taj put on their ski clothes. "Time for school!" Zoe says.

1. When does the family get to their hotel?
- (A) late at night
- (B) before dinner
- (C) the next morning

2. Zoe says that it is time for school. What does she mean?
- (A) They are going to do their homework.
- (B) They are going to learn how to ski.
- (C) They are going to learn how to ice skate.

2. Which clue in the text tells you that Zoe is excited for ski school?

_____

_____

_____

_____

© Shell Education   135043—180 Days of Reading   55

Name: _____   Date: _____

As You Read Underline something that is fun or interesting. Share it with a friend or adult.

Ski School

Zoe and Taj take skiing lessons the first day. First, they learn how to get up after a fall. They fall down a lot. But it is still fun. That afternoon, they ride the ski lift to the top of a small hill. Soon they can zip down the hill without falling. They are skiers!

Directions: Read "Ski School." Answer the questions.

1. What do you think the girls will want to do the next day?

   (A) quit skiing

   (B) go back home

   (C) go skiing again

2. What is a ski lift?

   (A) seats that take skiers up a hill

   (B) an elevator that helps lift skis

   (C) a pair of skis and poles

3. Which is another good title for this text?

   (A) Learning to Ski

   (B) Learning to Snowboard

   (C) Learning to Play

4. Write three things that Zoe and Taj do at ski school.

1.	
2.	
3.	

Name: _____ Date: _____

Directions: Reread "Ski School." Respond to the prompt.

Think about how a ski lesson might be helpful. What if Zoe and Taj did not take a lesson? How might their day be different? **Write** about what you think would happen. **Draw** a picture.

Kids Ski Lessons

Sign Up Now!

Ages 8–12

Two-day camp for $300
- Have Fun and Exercise
- Learn Skiing Basics
- Master the Bunny Slopes
- Enjoy Free Hot Chocolate!

All Levels Welcome

Saturdays and Sundays All Winter

Adventure Mountain, Vermont

Name: _____ Date: _____

Directions: Read "Kids Ski Lessons." Answer the questions.

1. What can you learn from reading this flyer?
   - (A) Ski lessons are free.
   - (B) Adventure Mountain is in Vermont.
   - (C) The camp is three days.

2. Who should **not** sign-up to take these lessons?
   - (A) a twelve-year-old
   - (B) an eight-year-old
   - (C) a mom

3. Which picture shows a word that ends with the same two sounds as *learn*?
   - (A)
   - (B)
   - (C)

4. Which information on the flyer do you think is most important? Why?

   _____

   _

   _____

   _

   _____

   _

   _____

Directions: Read the text. Study the flyer on page 59. Look for words about skiing in each text. Circle the words. Use three of the words to write your own sentences.

Close-Reading Text

Ski School

Zoe and Taj take skiing lessons the first day. First, they learn how to get up after a fall. They fall down a lot. But it is still fun. That afternoon, they ride the ski lift to the top of a small hill. Soon they can zip down the hill without falling. They are skiers!

1. _____

_____

2. _____

_____

3. _____

_____

Name: _____ Date: _____

Directions: Read the text. Study the flyer on page 59. Write what the texts are mostly about on the chart.

Close-Reading Text

The Snurfer
Sherman Poppen had made a great toy. It needed a name. His wife called it a snurfer. Soon a toy company started making them. Lots of children used them for a few years. Later, people thought of ways to make them better. You may have used what came next: the snowboard!

The Snurfer	
Kids Ski Lessons	

Name: _____ Date: _____

Directions: Think about the texts from this unit. Respond to the prompt.

You are writing a letter to a friend about ski school. You want them to go to ski school with you. **Tell** them why they should go with you. **Draw** a picture.

_____

_ _ _ _ _ _ _ _ _ _ _ _ _ _

_____,

_____

_ _ _ _ _ _ _ _ _ _ _ _ _ _ _

_____

_ _ _ _ _ _ _ _ _ _ _ _ _ _ _

_____

_____

_ _ _ _ _ _ _ _ _ _ _ _ _ _ _

_____

_____

_ _ _ _ _ _ _ _ _ _ _ _

_____

Name: _____ Date: _____

Directions: Reread "Kids Ski Lessons." Then, respond to the prompt.

Imagine you are in a play. The name of the play is "Goldilocks and the Three Bears." **Design** a flyer for the play. Give details about the event. **Draw** pictures on the flyer to show people what the play is about.

Name: _____ Date: _____

Directions: Read the text. Answer the questions.

As You Read ⟩ Underline what Mr. Crum does with potatoes.

Mr. Crum's Potatoes

George Crum lived long ago. He was a good chef. He worked in a restaurant. He liked to make a potato dish. He would slice potatoes and fry them.

1. What did Mr. Crum do?
- (A) cook potatoes
- (B) grow potatoes
- (C) mash potatoes

2. What is something Mr. Crum did **not** do to the potatoes?
- (A) slice them
- (B) bake them
- (C) fry them

3. What does a *chef* do?
- (A) paint pictures
- (B) cook food
- (C) build houses

Name: _____ Date: _____

Directions: Read the text. Answer the questions.

As You Read ⟩ Underline why the man doesn't like the potatoes.

More Potatoes

One diner asked for the fried potatoes. Mr. Crum made them for him. But the man did not like them. He said the potato slices were too thick.

1. What did the man want to eat?
- (A) potato salad
- (B) fried potatoes
- (C) a baked potato

2. Why did the man not like the potatoes?
- (A) He wanted the potatoes to be thinner.
- (B) He was not that hungry.
- (C) He did not want them fried.

3. Which word ends with the same sound as *thick*?

(A)   (B)   (C)

Name: _____ Date: _____

Directions: Read the text. Answer the questions.

As You Read ⟩ Underline how Mr. Crum felt.

Crisp Potatoes

Mr. Crum was annoyed. He thought he would teach the man a lesson. So, he sliced the potatoes very thin. They were thinner than he had ever sliced them. Then, he fried them until they were crisp.

1. How does Mr. Crum change the potatoes?

(A) He makes them cold and hard.

(B) He makes them thin and crisp.

(C) He makes them thick and crisp.

2. What does the word *crisp* mean?

(A) crunchy   (B) hot   (C) soft

3. What is Mr. Crum's problem? What does he do to solve it?

_____

_ _

_____

_ _

_____

As You Read › Underline information that is new or interesting. Circle the word with three syllables.

A Basket of Crisps

George Crum got a big surprise. The diner liked the "crisps." He asked for more. Soon, other diners asked for them.

A few years later, Mr. Crum had his own restaurant. All diners got crisps in a basket. You may have had these crisps, too. Today, they are known as potato chips!

Name: _____ Date: _____

Unit 4
WEEK 1
DAY
4

Directions: Read "A Basket of Crisps." Answer the questions.

1. Why do you think the potatoes were first called *crisps*?
   - (A) They were hard and thick.
   - (B) They were soft and thin.
   - (C) They were thin and crunchy.

2. How did Mr. Crum serve the crisps?
   - (A) on a plate
   - (B) in a basket
   - (C) in a bag

3. Why was Mr. Crum surprised?
   - (A) He did not like the crisps.
   - (B) He did not think the diner would like the crisps.
   - (C) He did not want to make the crisps.

4. Trace the topic. Write two facts about crisps.

Crisps

© Shell Education135043—180 Days of Reading69

Name: _____ Date: _____

Directions: Reread "A Basket of Crisps." Respond to the prompt.

Imagine you are Mr. Crum. You want people to try your restaurant and crisps. **Design** an advertisement. Make sure to give details about the restaurant and crisps. **Draw** pictures on the sign.

Name: _____ Date: _____

Directions: Read the text. Answer the questions.

As You Read ⟩ Underline words that tell what Erin found.

Prize Winner

It was a normal day for Erin. She was eating lunch with her friends. She opened a bag of chips. She saw something in the bag.

She pulled it out slowly. It was a letter. It said she had won a special prize! She couldn't believe it!

1. How does Erin feel after she reads the letter?

Ⓐ sad

Ⓑ surprised

Ⓒ scared

2. Who is Erin eating lunch with?

Ⓐ her friends

Ⓑ her sister

Ⓒ her mom

3. Which words are in correct alphabetical order?

Ⓐ chips, prize, special

Ⓑ special, chips, prize

Ⓒ chips, special, prize

Directions: Read the text. Answer the questions.

> **As You Read** | Underline what the winners get to do.

The Prize Details

Erin showed her mom the letter. They called the phone number in the letter. A nice woman picked up. She said the winners would get to eat potato chips. They would answer questions about the chips. Then, they would each get $50!

"Sounds great to me!" Erin said. "I would have done it for free!"

1. How does Erin know who to call?

  (A) Her mother gives her the number.

  (B) There is a number in the letter.

  (C) There is a number on the bag of chips.

2. What does Erin say she would do for free?

  (A) write a letter

  (B) make a phone call

  (C) eat chips and answer questions

3. Which word has the same beginning sound as *phone*?

  (A) poor   (B) find   (C) poof

Name: _____ Date: _____

Directions: Read the text. Answer the questions.

As You Read Underline describing words.

Taste Tester

It was the big day! Erin went inside a big building with her mom. She met the other people who won the prize, too.

The group was led into a room where they tasted a few chip flavors. Erin thought they all tasted great. She made some new friends, too.

1. What is the setting?

Ⓐ a grocery store

Ⓑ a school

Ⓒ inside a big building

2. What is Erin's job?

Ⓐ making new friends

Ⓑ tasting chips

Ⓒ winning a prize

3. Does Erin have a good day? How do you know?

_____

_____

_____

_____

Name: _____ Date: _____

A Sweet Ending

It was the last day of taste testing. Erin and the group got to eat a bunch of chips. They also tasted a new chip flavor. They were supposed to come up with a name for the new flavor.

"Salty Sunshine!" Erin said. The group agreed!

Then, it was time to go.

"What will you do with the prize money?" Erin's mom asked. "Buy more chips?"

Erin laughed. "I won't be eating another chip for a while," she said. "But I could go for a smoothie! Let's go celebrate!"

Directions: Read "A Sweet Ending." Answer the questions.

1. When does this text take place?

(A) after Erin and her mom get smoothies

(B) the first day of taste testing

(C) the last day of taste testing

2. Why does Erin say she won't be eating another chip for a while?

(A) She doesn't like chips.

(B) She tasted many kinds of chips.

(C) Her mother doesn't want her to eat chips.

3. Which word is a compound word?

(A) sunshine

(B) won't

(C) testing

4. Describe the beginning, middle, and end of the text.

Beginning	
Middle	
End	

Name: _____ Date: _____

Directions: Reread "A Sweet Ending." Respond to the prompt.

Imagine that you are Erin. **Write** about her last day. Tell about it from her point of view. You may add new details. **Draw** a picture.

_____

- -

_____

- -

_____

- -

_____

- -

_____

- -

_____

Potato Chip Recipe

Ingredients

- 7 peeled potatoes
- 5 tsp. of salt
- 2 tsp. garlic powder
- 1 tsp. pepper
- oil

Steps

Step 1: Fill a bowl with ice water and salt. Slice the potatoes very thin. Put them in the bowl. Soak them for 30 minutes.

Step 2: Place them on paper towels. Pat them dry. Put the spices in a small bowl.

Step 3: Pour oil in a pan. Heat the oil. Fry the potatoes. Be sure they are golden brown.

Step 4: Take out the potatoes. Put them on paper towels. Let them dry. Put them in a large bowl. Pour in the spices. Toss the potatoes to cover them in the spices.

Step 5: Serve and enjoy!

Name: _____ Date: _____

Directions: Read "Potato Chip Recipe." Answer the questions.

1. What should you soak the potatoes in?
   - (A) oil
   - (B) garlic powder
   - (C) ice water and salt

2. Which step comes right after you fry the potatoes?
   - (A) Take out the potatoes.
   - (B) Pat the potatoes dry.
   - (C) Heat the oil.

3. Which word has the same *c* sound as the first sound in *circus*?
   - (A) combine
   - (B) recipe
   - (C) batch

4. Which parts of the recipe do you think would be hard to do? Why?

   _____
   _____
   _____
   _____
   _____
   _____

Name: _____ Date: _____

Directions: Read these texts. Write one way a character or thing changes in each text.

Close-Reading Texts

A Basket of Crisps	Taste Tester
The diner liked the "crisps." He asked for more. Soon, other diners asked for them. A few years later, Mr. Crum had his own restaurant. All diners got crisps in a basket. You may have had these crisps, too. Today, they are known as potato chips!	Erin went inside a big building with her mom. She met the other people who won the prize, too. The group was led into a room where they tasted a few chip flavors. Erin thought they all tasted great. She made some new friends, too.

Text	Changes
A Basket of Crisps	_____ _____ _____ _____ _____
Taste Tester	_____ _____ _____ _____

Name: _____ **Date:** _____

Directions: Read these texts. Look for words that describe chips. They can be action words. Write them in the chart.

Close-Reading Texts

Crisp Potatoes	Potato Chip Recipe
Mr. Crum was annoyed. He thought he would teach the man a lesson. So, he sliced the potatoes very thin. They were thinner than he had ever sliced them. Then, he fried them until they were crisp.	**Step 1:** Fill a bowl with ice water and salt. Slice the potatoes very thin. Put them in the bowl. Soak them for 30 minutes. **Step 3:** Pour oil in a pan. Heat the oil. Fry the potatoes. Be sure they are golden brown.

Text	Words About Chips
Crisp Potatoes	
Potato Chip Recipe	

135043—180 Days of Reading © Shell Education

Directions: Think about the texts in this unit. Respond to the prompt.

You are a food writer for a newspaper. You eat at Mr. Crum's restaurant. You try his crisps. **Write** a food review. Tell what the crisps taste like. Tell what you think about them. **Draw** a picture.

Review of Mr. Crum's Restaurant

Name: _____ Date: _____

Directions: Reread "Potato Chip Recipe." Respond to the prompt.

You are cooking a food that you enjoy. What ingredients will you need? What are the steps to make the food? **Write** the recipe on the card. **Draw** a picture.

How to make _____

_____

_____

_____

_____

_____

_____

_____

_____

Name: _____ Date: _____

Directions: Read the text. Answer the questions.

| As You Read | Underline words that describe what firefighters do. |

A Tough Job

Firefighters have tough jobs. They keep people safe. They need to be strong and brave. They put out fires. They run into burning buildings. They rescue people inside. They also rescue pets.

They wear special uniforms to do this. The uniforms protect them from the heat.

1. Which phrase does not describe a firefighter's job?

(A) rescue pets

(B) run into buildings

(C) arrest people

2. Why do firefighters wear special uniforms?

(A) They help to keep them safe.

(B) They look good.

(C) They are easy to clean.

3. Which word has the same vowel sound as *need*?

(A)   (B)   (C)

Name: _____ Date: _____

Directions: Read the text. Answer the questions.

As You Read > Underline the gear firefighters use.

Firefighter Gear

Firefighters have a lot of heavy gear! Their helmets are hard. They protect them from falling objects. They have axes. These help them break down doors. Their boots are very thick. They protect their feet from glass and metal. And they also wear air tanks on their backs. These help them breathe in smoky buildings.

1. Why do firefighters need to be strong?
   - Ⓐ They need to watch out for falling objects.
   - Ⓑ Their gear is heavy.
   - Ⓒ They must wear a helmet.

2. How do thick boots help firefighters?
   - Ⓐ They protect their feet from glass and metal.
   - Ⓑ They look good with their uniforms.
   - Ⓒ They boots make them run faster.

3. What does the word *gear* mean in this text?
   - Ⓐ wheels that help make a machine work
   - Ⓑ things firefighters wear and use
   - Ⓒ how fast a fire truck can go

135043—180 Days of Reading   © Shell Education

Directions: Read the text. Answer the questions.

As You Read > Underline the parts of a firetruck.

Help Is on the Way

A firetruck is big and red. It has loud sirens that tell people that help is on the way. The truck has a hose to spray water. This helps put out fires. The truck also has a tall ladder. The ladder is used to get into tall buildings.

1. What do firefighters do with the hose on the firetruck?

   Ⓐ get into tall buildings

   Ⓑ tell people that help is on the way

   Ⓒ spray water

2. Which word in the text describes the ladder and buildings?

   Ⓐ loud   Ⓑ tall   Ⓒ big

3. What is the main idea of this text?

   _____

   _

   _____

   _

   _____

As You Read › Underline a fact that is new or interesting. Circle the words with two syllables.

At the Fire Station

Firefighters work long hours. Many work overnight. They stay at the fire station. They might cook or eat meals together. If there is a fire, they need to act fast!

They put on their uniforms. They jump into the truck. They drive to the fire. Then, they will spray water on the fire. They will go inside to save people.

Name: _____ Date: _____

Unit 5
WEEK 1
DAY
4

Directions: Read "At the Fire Station." Answer the questions.

1. Why might firefighters cook or eat meals together?

   Ⓐ They live at the fire station.

   Ⓑ They have to be ready for a fire at any time.

   Ⓒ They need to put on their uniforms.

2. Which things happen at the fire station?

   Ⓐ going inside to save people

   Ⓑ spraying water on a fire

   Ⓒ putting on uniforms and jumping in the truck

3. *Firefighters* is a compound word. It is made of two smaller words: *fire* and *fighters*. Which word is also a compound word?

   Ⓐ station   Ⓑ uniforms   Ⓒ overnight

4. Trace the word. Write three facts about what firefighters do when there is a fire.

	Firefighters
1.	
2.	
3.	

© Shell Education   135043—180 Days of Reading   87

Name: _____ Date: _____

Directions: Reread "At the Fire Station." Respond to the prompt.

Imagine you are a firefighter asleep at the station. The alarm goes off. **Write** about what you think, feel, and do. Tell how you get ready to go fight a fire. **Draw** a picture.

_____

_____

_____

_____

_____

_____

Name: _____ Date: _____

Directions: Read the text. Answer the questions.

As You Read > Underline what dad says about the fire.

Flynn's Camping Trip

Flynn was excited to go camping. He went with his family. They drove to a forest. They unpacked the car. Then, Flynn's dad asked him to find sticks. His dad used them to build a fire. His dad said fire can be dangerous. Fire is very hot. He said Flynn had to be careful near it.

1. Which sentence is true?
   - (A) Flynn doesn't want to go camping.
   - (B) Flynn finds sticks for the campfire.
   - (C) They go camping at the beach.

2. What is the correct order of events?
   - (A) finding sticks, unpacking the car
   - (B) building a fire, driving to the forest
   - (C) unpacking the car, finding sticks

3. Who is telling the story?
   - (A) a narrator
   - (B) Flynn's father
   - (C) Flynn

Name: _____ Date: _____

Directions: Read the text. Answer the questions.

As You Read ⟩ Underline words that tell about the setting.

A Great Night

Flynn's family sat around the campfire. It was chilly, but the fire made them feel warm. They sang songs. They made s'mores. They all had a great night. When it was time for bed, Flynn and his family slept in sleeping bags inside tents. Flynn liked camping!

1. Where does the family sleep?
   - (A) in sleeping bags in the car
   - (B) in sleeping bags inside tents
   - (C) in sleeping bags under the stars

2. What is the purpose of this text?
   - (A) to tell what the family did at night
   - (B) to tell how to make s'mores
   - (C) to tell how to sing camp songs

3. What does the word *chilly* mean in the text?
   - (A) hungry
   - (B) cold
   - (C) funny

Directions: Read the text. Answer the questions.

> **As You Read** Underline what the family does on the hike.

More Camping Fun

The next day, Flynn's family woke up. They made another fire. They cooked eggs and bacon. Then, they went on a hike. Flynn's mom said a hike is a walk in nature. They listened for animals. They looked at the beautiful trees. Flynn loved it. It was fun but tiring!

1. Why does Flynn's family make another fire?

   Ⓐ It is very cold.

   Ⓑ They don't have anything else to do.

   Ⓒ They need to cook breakfast.

2. Which word has a silent *t* like in *listened*?

   Ⓐ castle   Ⓑ beautiful   Ⓒ tiring

3. What else do you think Flynn and his family saw on their hike?

_____

_____

_____

_____

Name: _____ Date: _____

Underline something that is interesting.
Circle action words with *-ing* endings.

Beware of Wildfires

Flynn and his family kept hiking. They started to smell smoke. On the trail, they met a park ranger. The ranger said there was a wildfire. The wildfire had caused a lot of trees to catch on fire. The ranger said the fire wasn't close to them. But wildfires are fast. They can spread quickly. The ranger said the family should leave the forest.

Flynn was sad. He wanted to keep camping. But his parents said staying safe is more important. They would plan another trip soon!

135043—180 Days of Reading   © Shell Education

Name: _____ Date: _____

Directions: Read "Beware of Wildfires." Answer the questions.

1. What causes the family to stop their camping trip?
   - (A) They are hiking in the wrong place.
   - (B) A wildfire has started.
   - (C) The fire is about to burn their tent.

2. Which is another good title for this text?
   - (A) "Wildfire Danger"
   - (B) "Beware of Hiking"
   - (C) "A Fun Camping Trip"

3. The word important has three syllables: *im–por–tant*. Which word also has three syllables?
   - (A) ranger
   - (B) camping
   - (C) another

4. Describe the beginning, middle, and end of the text.

Beginning	
Middle	
End	

Name: _____ Date: _____

Directions: Reread "Beware of Wildfires." Respond to the prompt.

Imagine you are the park ranger. **Write** what you would say to Flynn's family as the park ranger. Tell them what is happening. Tell them what they should do. **Draw** a picture.

_____

_____

_____

_____

_____

_____

_____

What Am I?

I live between the sidewalk and the street,

Sometimes on grass; sometimes on concrete.

I can be yellow but am usually red.

I am not a living thing, but I'm also not dead.

There's no parking near me with your car.

Drivers, find another spot, whether near or far!

Firefighters hook up their hoses as fast as
they can.

I provide the water to save buildings and land.

At least, that's the plan!

What am I?

Name: _____ Date: _____

Directions: Read "What Am I?" Answer the questions.

1. Which is a clue from the poem?

   (A) "I can be yellow..."

   (B) "...that's the plan!"

   (C) "...as fast as they can"

2. What is the answer to the question: *Who am I?*

   (A) a sidewalk

   (B) a fire hose

   (C) a fire hydrant

3. Who is speaking in the poem?

   (A) a fire hose

   (B) a fire hydrant

   (C) a firefighter

4. Which clues did you find the most useful in the poem? Why?

   _____

   -

   _____

   _____

   -

   _____

   _____

   -

   _____

Directions: Read these texts. Look for words or phrases about fires. Underline them. Use three of the words or phrases to write your own sentences.

Close-Reading Texts

Flynn's Camping Trip	What Am I?
Then, Flynn's dad asked him to find sticks. His dad used them to build a fire. His dad said fire can be dangerous. Fire is very hot. He said Flynn had to be careful near it.	Drivers, find another spot, whether near or far! Firefighters hook up their hoses as fast as they can. I provide the water to save buildings and land. At least, that's the plan! What am I?

1. _____

2. _____

3. _____

Name: _____ Date: _____

Directions: Read these texts. Write an effect for each cause on the charts.

Close-Reading Texts

A Great Night

Flynn's family sat around the campfire. It was chilly, but the fire made them feel warm. They sang songs. They made s'mores. They all had a great night. When it was time for bed, Flynn and his family slept in sleeping bags inside tents. Flynn liked camping!

Cause

The family built a fire at the camp.

Effect

Beware of Wildfires

The ranger said there was a wildfire. The wildfire had caused a lot of trees to catch on fire. The ranger said the fire wasn't close to them. But wildfires are fast. They can spread quickly. The ranger said the family should leave the forest.

Cause

There was a wildfire.

Effect

Name: _____ Date: _____

Directions: Think about the texts in this unit. Respond to the prompt.

Write a poem about fire. Use ideas from the texts. You can also add your own ideas. Trace the title. Complete each line in the poem. **Draw** a picture.

Example: Fire is *sometimes wild*.

Fire

Fire is _____.

Fire is _____.

Fire can _____.

Fire can _____.

Fire can _____.

Name: _____ Date: _____

Directions: Reread "What Am I?" Respond to the prompt.

Write three clues about an object. **Write** the name of the object on the bottom line. **Draw** the object in the box. **Read** the clues to a friend or adult. Have them guess the object!

What Am I?

_____

1. _____

2. _____

3. _____

_____

Name: _____ Date: _____

Directions: Read the text. Answer the questions.

As You Read > Underline where James worked.

Playing Indoors

James worked at a school. He was in charge of sports. He needed an inside sport for children to play during cold winters.

1. What did James do for his job?
   - (A) teach sports
   - (B) teach art
   - (C) teach math

2. What caused James to need an inside sport?
   - (A) It is more fun to play inside.
   - (B) It is too hot to play outside.
   - (C) It is too cold to play outside.

3. What does the phrase *in charge of sports* mean?
   - (A) be responsible for sports
   - (B) like to watch sports
   - (C) play sports

Name: _____ Date: _____

Directions: Read the text. Answer the questions.

As You Read 〉 Make a prediction about what you think happens next.

James Had an Idea

James wanted a game that could be played in a small space. He got a soccer ball. He got two peach baskets. Then, he wrote some rules.

1. What did James do?
   - Ⓐ play soccer until lunchtime
   - Ⓑ gather supplies to make a game
   - Ⓒ put peaches in baskets

2. What did James get for the game?
   - Ⓐ two peach baskets and two soccer balls
   - Ⓑ two peach baskets and one baseball
   - Ⓒ two peach baskets and one soccer ball

3. Which is the word for the number 2?
   - Ⓐ to
   - Ⓑ two
   - Ⓒ too

Directions: Read the text. Answer the questions.

> **As You Read** > Underline where the baskets are.

A Big Problem

James had tied each basket high up on a railing. Each team tried to get the ball into the basket. But there was a big problem!

1. What did each team want to do?
   - (A) hit the basket with the ball
   - (B) knock the basket down with the ball
   - (C) get the ball in the basket

2. Which word has the same vowel sound as *there*?
   - (A) these
   - (B) their
   - (C) they

3. What do you think was the problem? How could James solve it?

   _____

   _ _ _ _ _ _ _ _ _ _ _ _ _ _ _ _ _ _

   _____

   _ _ _ _ _ _ _ _ _ _ _ _ _ _ _ _ _ _

Name: _____   Date: _____

As You Read > Underline something that is new or interesting. Share it with a friend or adult.

A New Game

James called his game *basketball*. At first, players had to toss the ball back and forth to get to the baskets. Years later, the rules changed. Players could dribble the ball as they ran.

The basket problem got solved, too. A hoop with a net replaced each peach basket. The ball could swish right through the tall hoop. Basketball was a hit!

Directions: Read "A New Game." Answer the questions.

1. How did the game of basketball change over time?

(A) It went from peach baskets to apple baskets.

(B) It went from only tossing the ball to dribbling the ball as well.

(C) It went from being fun to being hard.

2. Which is another good title for this text?

(A) How to Dribble a Ball

(B) How to Solve a Problem

(C) The Beginnings of Basketball

3. Why is a hoop with a net better than a basket?

(A) Players do not have to get the ball out of the basket.

(B) Players do not get to rest as much.

(C) Players can shoot the ball better.

4. Trace the words. Write two changes that were made to the game.

Rule Changes

1. _____

2. _____

Name: _____ Date: _____

Directions: Reread "A New Game." Respond to the prompt.

Think about how basketball changed. How might you change a different sport? How could you make it easier or harder? What would make it more fun? Write about your favorite sport and tell how you could change it. **Draw** a picture.

_____

- -

_____

- -

_____

- -

_____

- -

_____

- -

_____

Name: _____ Date: _____

Directions: Read the text. Answer the questions.

As You Read ⟩ Underline what Zoe says she will do for free.

A New Sport

Zoe held up a basketball camp poster.

"Since when do you want to play basketball?" Zoe's mom asked.

"Since all my friends started playing!" Zoe said. "Can I go to this camp? I'll do any chores you need for free!"

"Let's start with doing your homework," Zoe's mom said, laughing.

1. Why does Zoe want to play basketball?
   - (A) Her friends have started playing.
   - (B) It is one of her chores.
   - (C) Her mother wants her to play.

2. What does Zoe's mom want her to do?
   - (A) her chores
   - (B) her homework
   - (C) play with her friends

3. What does the word *chores* mean?
   - (A) homework
   - (B) sports
   - (C) jobs

Name: _____ Date: _____

Directions: Read the text. Answer the questions.

As You Read ⟩ Underline what Zoe learned to do.

Zoe's First Basket

Zoe was nervous when camp started. She had never played basketball before. She thought the game looked fun. But it also looked really hard.

First, the coach taught her group how to dribble. Then, they practiced shooting the ball. Soon, Zoe made her first basket!

1. How does Zoe feel at the beginning of camp?

Ⓐ scared

Ⓑ angry

Ⓒ nervous

2. Which shows the correct order of activities for Zoe?

Ⓐ shooting, dribbling, making a basket

Ⓑ dribbling, shooting, making a basket

Ⓒ making a basket, dribbling, shooting

3. Which word has the same vowel sound as *thought*?

Ⓐ few

Ⓑ looked

Ⓒ saw

135043—180 Days of Reading

Name: _____ Date: _____

Directions: Read the text. Answer the questions.

> **As You Read** Underline how Zoe's arms felt.

Passing Drills

Zoe's group at camp learned how to pass the basketball. First, they learned bounce passes. They bounced the ball between themselves. They also learned chest passes. Zoe loved the passing drills! But her arms were very sore the next day.

1. What new skills does Zoe learn at this practice?

   (A) running and passing

   (B) passing and dribbling

   (C) bounce passing and chest passing

2. Why are Zoe's arms sore the next day?

   (A) She fell down and hurt them.

   (B) She uses them to practice passing at practice.

   (C) She gets hit with the basketball.

3. Based on what they are called, what is the difference between a bounce pass and a chest pass?

_____

_ _

_____

_ _

_____

Name: _____   Date: _____

As You Read Try to make a connection to the text. Underline where you make a connection. Share it with a friend or adult.

Game Time!

Zoe played her first basketball game at camp. She played the position of point guard. She had to dribble the ball up the court. Toward the end of the game, the score was tied. The coach called a time out and gave the team tips on how to win.

They got back on the court. Zoe passed the ball to her teammate. She shot it and scored! Zoe's team won the game!

Zoe knew she still had a lot of basketball skills to learn. But after this camp, she wasn't nervous to try new sports anymore.

Name: _____ Date: _____

Directions: Read "Game Time!" Answer the questions.

1. How does Zoe help her team win?
   - Ⓐ She passes the ball to a teammate.
   - Ⓑ She scores the winning basket.
   - Ⓒ She calls a time out.

2. Which sentence is true?
   - Ⓐ Zoe is scared to try more sports.
   - Ⓑ Zoe knows she is the best basketball player.
   - Ⓒ Zoe plays her first basketball game at camp.

3. What does *time out* mean in this text?
   - Ⓐ making a player sit out of the game
   - Ⓑ giving the ball to the other team
   - Ⓒ stopping the game for a short amount of time

4. Number the sentences 1, 2, 3, or 4 to put them in the correct order.

	The score was tied.
	Zoe passed the ball to her teammate.
	The coach called a time out.
	Zoe's team won the game.

Name: _____ Date: _____

Directions: Reread "Game Time!" Respond to the prompt.

Think about what Zoe did to help her team win the game. **Write** about a time when you helped someone or worked with others like Zoe did. **Draw** a picture.

Name: _____ Date: _____

Is It for Me?

There's a wrapped present under the tree,

I know it must be for me.

It's round and hard,

But there's no card.

I sneak down late at night

To look at this gift in the dim light.

It can roll on the floor.

Is it something I adore?

One more test before I go!

Yes! I can bounce it, dribble, and throw.

A basketball! How did they know?!

Name: _____ Date: _____

Directions: Read "Is It For Me?" Answer the questions.

1. When does this poem take place?
   - (A) by the Christmas tree
   - (B) late at night during Christmas
   - (C) on Christmas day

2. Why does the boy think the present is for him?
   - (A) He wants a basketball.
   - (B) The card has his name on it.
   - (C) The present bounces.

3. What does *adore* mean?
   - (A) a test
   - (B) something that bounces
   - (C) to love

4. What words does the author use to describe the present? List five of them.

   _____   _____

   _____, _____,

   _____, _____,

   _____

Directions: Read these texts. Look for basketball words in each text. Write the words on the chart.

Close-Reading Texts

A New Game	Game Time!
James called his game *basketball*. At first, players had to toss the ball back and forth to get to the baskets. Years later, the rules changed. Players could dribble the ball as they ran.	Zoe played her first basketball game at camp. She played the position of point guard. She had to dribble the ball up the court. Toward the end of the game, the score was tied. The coach called a time out and gave the team tips on how to win.

Basketball Words

A New Game	Game Time!

Name: _____ Date: _____

Directions: Read the text. Then, reread "Is It For Me?"
Record details about each text in the charts.

Close-Reading Text

Passing Drills
Zoe's group at camp learned how to pass the basketball. First, they learned bounce passes. They bounced the ball between themselves. They also learned chest passes. Zoe loved the passing drills! But her arms were very sore the next day.

Passing Drills

Characters	Setting	Event

Is It for Me?

Characters	Setting	Event

Name: _____ Date: _____

Directions: Reread "Zoe's First Basket." Respond to the prompt.

Imagine you are Zoe. You have just finished your first day at basketball camp. **Write** a diary entry about your day. Tell what you did and how you felt. **Draw** a picture.

_____

_____

_____

_____

_____

_____

Name: _____ Date: _____

Directions: Reread "Is It for Me?" Respond to the prompt.

Think of a present you would like to get. **Write** words in the blanks. Finish the poem. **Draw** the present. **Read** the poem to a friend or adult.

Is It for Me?

There's a wrapped present under the tree,

I know it must be for me.

_____   _____

_ _ _ _ _ _ _ _ _   _ _ _ _ _ _ _ _ _

It's _____ and _____,

And there's no card.

I sneak down late at night

To look at this gift in the light.

_____

_ _ _ _ _ _ _ _ _ _ _

It can _____ on the floor.

Is it something I adore?

One more test before I go.

_____

_ _ _ _ _ _ _ _ _ _

It _____!

_____

_ _ _ _ _ _ _ _ _

It's a _____!

How did they know?!

Directions: Read the text. Answer the questions.

As You Read > Underline what service dogs do.

Service Dogs

Some dogs have important jobs. They are called *service dogs*. Some service dogs are trained to help people who are blind or deaf. They help keep their owners safe.

1. What kind of dog is this text about?
   - (A) pet dogs
   - (B) sled dogs
   - (C) service dogs

2. What might a service dog do to help?
   - (A) walk someone across the street
   - (B) play with other dogs in the park
   - (C) whine to be petted

3. What does the word *trained* mean in this text?
   - (A) worked
   - (B) taught
   - (C) helped

Name: _____ Date: _____

Directions: Read the text. Answer the questions.

As You Read Underline how service dogs can help people who are deaf.

Special Duties

Some service dogs help people who are deaf. They are trained to react to sounds. Did the doorbell just ring? The dog will touch its owner to let them know. The dog can also wake up a person if an alarm goes off.

1. What does the text say a service dog can do?
   - (A) sing
   - (B) ring a doorbell
   - (C) help a person who is deaf

2. How does the dog tell something to a person who is deaf?
   - (A) It barks loudly at the person.
   - (B) It touches the person.
   - (C) It jumps onto the person.

3. Which word has the same vowel sound as *deaf*?

   (A)   (B)   (C)

Name: _____ Date: _____

Directions: Read the text. Answer the questions.

As You Read ⟩ Underline how service dogs can help people who use wheelchairs.

More Ways to Help

Some service dogs help people who use wheelchairs. They can turn lights on and off. They can pick up books. They can even open and close doors.

1. Which sentence is **not** true?

   Ⓐ Service dogs can turn lights on and off.

   Ⓑ Service dogs can use a wheelchair.

   Ⓒ Service dogs can pick up a book.

2. What does the word *service* mean in this text?

   Ⓐ helpful

   Ⓑ playful

   Ⓒ careful

3. What is the main idea of this text?

   _____

   _____

   _____

Name: _____ Date: _____

As You Read Underline something that is new or interesting. Share it with a friend or adult.

Dog Heroes

Has there been an earthquake? Did a bad storm hit? Did a hiker get lost on a mountain? When these events happen, some dogs go to work. They are called *search and rescue dogs*.

These dogs have a much better sense of smell than people have. These dogs have been trained to use their noses. They have found people buried under snow or buildings. These dogs are real heroes!

 135043—180 Days of Reading

Name: _____ Date: _____

Directions: Read "Dog Heroes." Answer the questions.

1. What does *search and rescue* mean?
   - (A) to dig up things
   - (B) to help people get around
   - (C) to look for and save people

2. Why are dogs good at searches?
   - (A) They like people.
   - (B) They have a good sense of smell.
   - (C) They have four legs.

3. Which word is spelled correctly?
   - (A) hereos
   - (B) heros
   - (C) heroes

4. Trace the words. Write three ways search and rescue dogs can help.

	Search and Rescue Dogs
1.	
2.	
3.	

Name: _____ Date: _____

Directions: Reread "Dog Heroes." Respond to the prompt.

Think about how dogs help people. How would you like a dog to help you? Would it help you cross the street? Would it do tricks that make you laugh? **Write** about what you would like a dog to do to help you. **Draw** a picture.

_____

_____

_____

_____

_____

_____

_____

_____

135043—180 Days of Reading   © Shell Education

Name: _____ Date: _____

Directions: Read the text. Answer the questions.

> **As You Read** > Underline the descriptions of Mac.

A New Student

There's a new student in my school named Mac. He is really nice, but he doesn't look like the other students. He has four legs and a wet nose. He's a service dog!

Mac helps detect when there are nuts in our school. Many kids are allergic to nuts. His job is to protect them.

1. Is Mac a student?

   (A) Yes, and he is allergic to nuts.

   (B) No, he is a service dog.

   (C) No, he is a new teacher.

2. What does Mac detect?

   (A) students who are allergic to nuts

   (B) people who eat nuts

   (C) nuts at school

3. What does *there's* mean?

   (A) there is

   (B) there are

   (C) they are

Name: _____ Date: _____

Directions: Read the text. Answer the questions.

As You Read ⟩ Underline what Mac's trainer tells the students.

Serious Work

Mac's trainer is an officer in our school. He tells us that we cannot pet Mac when he is working. Mac needs to do his job. The trainer says that the best thing to do is ignore Mac. That helps him stay focused. But on field days, we get to play with Mac!

1. Why can't the students pet Mac when he is working?
    - (A) He needs to focus on his job.
    - (B) He might bite them.
    - (C) His trainer will get angry.

2. When do the students get to play with Mac?
    - (A) on holidays
    - (B) when they are doing their homework
    - (C) on field days

3. Which is the base word of *focused*?
    - (A) folks
    - (B) focusing
    - (C) focus

Name: _____ Date: _____

Name: _____ Date: _____

Unit 7 — WEEK 2 — DAY 3

Directions: Read the text. Answer the questions.

As You Read Underline what the narrator is excited to do.

Mac's Alert

Last week, we had a field day! I was excited for the games and races. But before we started the first race, Mac started barking near the snack table.

Mac's trainer went to the snack table. He found snacks on the table that had peanut butter.

"Good boy, Mac! You saved a life today," he said.

1. When did field day happen?
   - (A) yesterday
   - (B) last week
   - (C) today

2. Why does Mac bark at the snack table?
   - (A) He wants a snack.
   - (B) He is scared.
   - (C) He smells peanut butter.

3. What do you think will happen to the peanut butter snacks?

_____

_____

_____

_____

© Shell Education   135043—180 Days of Reading   127

Name: _____ Date: _____

As You Read ⟩ Underline a place where you can make a connection to the text. Share it with a friend or adult.

Field Day Hero

Field day was almost over. But a few students in my class got together. We talked about how we could thank Mac for his help. Then, we took our winning ribbons from the day and tied them together. It looked like one giant award. We wrote "Mac is our hero!" on it.

We gave it to Mac. Everyone hugged him. He wagged his tail and licked our hands.

Our principal heard the news. He hung the award up in our school. Now we can always remember Mac's big day!

Directions: Read "Field Day Hero." Answer the questions.

1. Why do the kids make Mac an award?
   - (A) They want to thank him.
   - (B) They want him to play with it.
   - (C) They don't want their awards.

2. Who hangs up the award at school?
   - (A) Mac's owner
   - (B) the teacher
   - (C) the principal

3. Which word correctly completes the sentence? I am _____ the picture.
   - (A) hanging
   - (B) hang
   - (C) hanged

4. Trace the words in the middle oval. Write words or phrases in the ovals that describe Mac's award.

Mac's Award

Name: _____ Date: _____

Directions: Reread "Field Day Hero." Respond to the prompt.

Think about why the students made an award for Mac. Who might you make and give an award to? **Draw** an award. **Label** the award. **Write** who the award is for. Write why you are giving it to them.

135043—180 Days of Reading   © Shell Education

Pup to the Rescue!

This dog is learning to rescue people.

He uses his great sense of smell to find people.

They might be trapped or hurt.

He trains every day.

One day, he might be a hero!

Name: _____ Date: _____

Directions: Read "Pup to the Rescue!" Answer the questions.

1. Why would a dog need to rescue people?
   - (A) People like to see dogs when they are scared.
   - (B) People think dogs are friendly.
   - (C) Dogs can smell people who are trapped or hurt.

2. Which is another good title for this text?
   - (A) "A Hero in Training"
   - (B) "All About Dogs"
   - (C) "Dogs are Nice"

3. What does the word *trains* mean in this text?
   - (A) toys
   - (B) practices
   - (C) follows

4. What might this dog do to become a hero?

   _____

   _ _ _ _ _ _ _ _ _ _ _ _ _ _ _ _ _ _ _

   _____

   _ _ _ _ _ _ _ _ _ _ _ _ _ _ _ _ _ _ _

   _____

   _ _ _ _ _ _ _ _ _ _ _ _ _ _ _ _ _ _ _

   _____

Name: _____ Date: _____

Directions: Read these texts. Complete the chart with information about the texts.

Close-Reading Texts

A New Student	Field Day Hero
There's a new student in my school named Mac. He is really nice, but he doesn't look like the other students. He has four legs and a wet nose. He's a service dog! Mac helps detect when there are nuts in our school. Many kids are allergic to nuts. His job is to protect them.	We talked about how we could thank Mac for his help. Then, we took our winning ribbons from the day and tied them together. It looked like one giant award. We wrote "Mac is our hero!" on it. We gave it to Mac. Everyone hugged him. He wagged his tail and licked our hands.

Information	A New Student	Field Day Hero
Characters		
One Key Detail		
Important Words		

Name: _____ Date: _____

Directions: Read these texts. Look for details about rescue dogs. Write them in the chart.

Close-Reading Texts

Dog Heroes	Pup to the Rescue!
They are called search and rescue dogs. These dogs have a much better sense of smell than people have. These dogs have been trained to use their noses. They have found people buried under snow or buildings. These dogs are real heroes!	This dog is learning to rescue people. He uses his great sense of smell to find people. They might be trapped or hurt. He trains every day. One day, he might be a hero!

Rescue Dog Details	
Dog Heroes	**Pup to the Rescue!**

Name: _____ Date: _____

Directions: Reread "Pup to the Rescue!" Respond to the prompt.

Draw pictures on the storyboard to go with the text. **Add** your own ending. **Share** the story with a friend.

Pup to the Rescue!

This dog is learning to rescue people.	He uses his great sense of smell to find people.
They might be trapped or hurt.	He trains every day.

_____

_ _ _ _ _ _ _ _ _ _ _ _ _ _ _ _

_____

Name: _____ Date: _____

Directions: Think about the texts from this unit. Respond to the prompt.

Think about Mac from "Field Day Hero." **Design** a magazine page to tell about Mac and what he does. **Draw** a picture.

Name: _____ Date: _____

Directions: Read the text. Answer the questions.

As You Read ⟩ Underline new or interesting facts.

What Is a Hurricane?

A hurricane is a huge storm. It begins over the ocean. The winds blow in a circle. The winds are super strong. They can blow hundreds of miles (kilometers) per hour. And it rains hard.

1. What is a hurricane?

(A) a storm that starts over land

(B) a storm that starts after it rains

(C) a storm that starts over water

2. Which sentence is true about hurricanes?

(A) Strong winds blow in a circle.

(B) Light winds blow across the ocean.

(C) Strong winds can blow 300 miles per hour.

3. The word *hurricane* has three syllables: *hur–ri–cane*. Which word also has three syllables?

(A) alligator

(B) hammer

(C) grasshopper

Name: _____ Date: _____

Directions: Read the text. Answer the questions.

> **As You Read** Circle new or important words.

The Eye

The center of a hurricane is called the *eye*. The winds do not blow as hard in the eye. It also does not rain as much in the eye.

eye

1. What is the *eye* of a hurricane?
   - (A) the outer edge of the storm
   - (B) the area where the storm starts
   - (C) the area in the middle of the storm

2. What is it like in the eye of a hurricane?
   - (A) The storm is quieter.
   - (B) The storm is windier.
   - (C) The storm is rainier.

3. Which word rhymes with *rain*?
   - (A) ring
   - (B) explain
   - (C) band

Name: _____ Date: _____

Directions: Read the text. Answer the questions.

As You Read ⟩ Underline new or interesting facts.

Hurricanes and the Ocean

Hurricane winds are strong. They push around water in the ocean. Giant waves start to form. The ocean level can get very high. This is called a storm surge. It can cause flooding.

1. What happens in a storm surge?

   Ⓐ The waves and ocean level get high.

   Ⓑ The waves get smaller.

   Ⓒ The waves make more wind and rain.

2. What pushes the waves in a hurricane?

   Ⓐ water

   Ⓑ wind

   Ⓒ rain

3. Why do you think the author wrote this text?

_____

_____

_____

_____

Name: _____ Date: _____

As You Read
Underline something that is new or interesting. Circle three important words.

A Hurricane on Land

Is a hurricane coming? Do you live near the ocean? Then you may need to leave home until the storm ends.

The strong winds can tear up trees. The rain can cause flooding. The ocean level may rise with the storm surge. Boats can get tossed around by the waves. The beach may get worn away. Be sure to go somewhere safe if a hurricane is coming.

Directions: Read "A Hurricane on Land." Answer the questions.

1. What kind of place would be safe in a hurricane?
   - Ⓐ a house by the beach
   - Ⓑ a house away from the beach
   - Ⓒ a park near the ocean

2. Why do some people have to leave home during a hurricane?
   - Ⓐ Being in a car is safer.
   - Ⓑ It is easier to watch a hurricane outside.
   - Ⓒ It may not be safe.

3. What is the main idea of this text?
   - Ⓐ A hurricane can be unsafe when it hits land.
   - Ⓑ A hurricane can be shown on TV.
   - Ⓒ A hurricane moves faster across land.

4. Trace the words. Write three facts about what can happen during a hurricane.

	Hurricane Facts
1.	
2.	
3.	

Name: _____ Date: _____

Directions: Reread "A Hurricane on Land." Respond to the prompt.

Think about what a beach looks like. What would it look like after a hurricane? **Write** what you might see on a beach after a big storm. **Draw** a picture.

_____

- -

_____

_____

_____

- -

_____

_____

- -

_____

Directions: Read the text. Answer the questions.

As You Read ▷ Underline how Mark feels.

A Storm Is Coming

"There's a hurricane coming," said Mark's dad.

"I'm scared," Mark said.

"There's no reason to be scared," Dad said. "We just have to prepare. Let's get flashlights in case the wind knocks the power out."

"Can we make a pillow fort too?" asked Mark.

"Of course!" said Mark's dad.

1. What might make the power go out at Mark's house?
- (A) winds from a hurricane
- (B) cold air from a snow storm
- (C) rain from a storm

2. Which word has the same beginning sound as *knocks*?
- (A) night
- (B) keeps
- (C) socks

3. What does *prepare* mean in this text?
- (A) to be scared
- (B) to get ready
- (C) to fix

Name: _____ Date: _____

Directions: Read the text. Answer the questions.

As You Read > Underline words that describe things.

Pillow Fort

The skies were dark and gray. The storm was coming soon. They closed all the windows. They found the safest place in their home. It was the hallway. It was far away from the windows. They made a fort with pillows and blankets. Mark's mom brought their favorite snacks. They were ready with their flashlights.

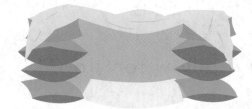

1. Why do they close all of the windows?
   - (A) It will keep the wind and rain out.
   - (B) It is night time.
   - (C) There is too much noise outside.

2. What do they use to make the fort?
   - (A) cushions from the couch
   - (B) a tent
   - (C) blankets and pillows

3. Which ending could be added to the root word *dark* to make a new word?
   - (A) *–ing*
   - (B) *–er*
   - (C) *–es*

Name: _____ Date: _____

Directions: Read the text. Answer the questions.

As You Read > Underline the dialogue (when someone is talking).

In the Dark

It was raining and windy outside. The lights started to flicker on and off. Then, it went dark. "Everything's okay!" said Mark's mom. "Let's turn on our flashlights."

The family played flashlight tag. They read books in the dark. After a while, the lights came back on.

"Can we turn them back off?" asked Mark. "I was having fun!"

1. When do the lights come back on?

    (A) before they turn on their flashlights

    (B) during flashlight tag

    (C) after reading books

2. Which part of the text tells the meaning of *flicker*?

    (A) go dark   (B) go on and off   (C) go brighter

3. How does Mark's family help him **not** worry during the storm?

_____

_____

_____

_____

Name: _____ Date: _____

Time to Help

After a few hours, the storm was over. Mark's town was safe, but towns near the ocean had a lot of damage. Some homes were flooded from the heavy rain. Kids lost clothes, books, and toys.

"This makes me sad," said Mark. "How can we help?"

"We can donate some things," Mark's mom said.

"What does that mean?" asked Mark.

"It's when you take things you have and give them to people who need them," Mark's mom said. So, Mark started making a pile of clothes he could donate.

Directions: Read "Time to Help." Answer the questions.

1. Which towns have damage from the hurricane?
   - (A) Mark's town
   - (B) mountain towns
   - (C) ocean towns

2. Why does Mark want to donate his clothes?
   - (A) They are too small.
   - (B) Other people need them.
   - (C) He wants to get new clothes.

3. Which word is spelled correctly?
   - (A) damage
   - (B) damege
   - (C) damadge

4. Write 1, 2, 3, 4, or 5 to put the events in the correct order.

	Mark says he is sad.
	Mark asks his mom what it means to donate.
	The hurricane is over.
	Mark starts going through his clothes.
	Mark's mom tells him they can donate.

Name: _____ Date: _____

Directions: Think about Mark's hurricane experience. Respond to the prompt.

Draw pictures of Mark before, during, and after the hurricane. **Write** a sentence describing how Mark's hurricane story ends.

Beginning	Middle	End

_____

- -

_____

- -

_____

Radio Weather Report

Welcome back, listeners! We hope you all are doing okay. It's 3:00 p.m. A hurricane hit our area about two hours ago. Many streets are flooded. Some homes don't have power. It looks like clear skies now. We're not supposed to get any rain tonight. Call us, and let us know how you are doing. What are you doing to stay calm? How did you and your family ride out the storm?

Name: _____ Date: _____

Directions: Read "Radio Weather Report." Answer the questions.

1. Why is it important that they are not supposed to get more rain?

   Ⓐ Some places are already flooded.

   Ⓑ The power is back on.

   Ⓒ It is 3 p.m. in the afternoon.

2. What can you learn from listening to this radio weather report?

   Ⓐ the temperature

   Ⓑ the date

   Ⓒ the time

3. What does *ride out* mean in the text?

   Ⓐ get out quickly

   Ⓑ ride a horse

   Ⓒ get through

4. How would you feel if you heard this report where you live? Why?

   _____

   _____

   _____

   _____

Name: _____ Date: _____

Directions: Read the text. Reread "Radio Weather Report." Answer the questions in the chart.

Close-Reading Text

Time to Help

After a few hours, the storm was over. Mark's town was safe, but towns near the ocean had a lot of damage. Some homes were flooded from the heavy rain. Kids lost clothes, books, and toys.

"This makes me sad," said Mark. "How can we help?"

"We can donate some things," Mark's mom said.

"What does that mean?" asked Mark.

"It's when you take things you have and give them to people who need them," Mark's mom said. So, Mark started making a pile of clothes he could donate.

Questions	Time to Help	Radio Weather Report
What is the setting?		
What does the main character want?		
What happens at the end?		

Name: _____ Date: _____

Directions: Read these texts. Underline words or phrases that describe what happens during a hurricane. Write them in the chart.

Close-Reading Texts

A Hurricane on Land	In the Dark
The strong winds can tear up trees. The rain can cause flooding. The ocean level may rise with the storm surge. Boats can get tossed around by the waves. The beach may get worn away. Be sure to go somewhere safe if a hurricane is coming.	It was raining and windy outside. The lights started to flicker on and off. Then, it went dark. "Everything's okay!" said Mark's mom. "Let's turn on our flashlights."

The family played flashlight tag. |

A Hurricane on Land	In the Dark

© Shell Education

Name: _____ Date: _____

Directions: Think about the texts from this unit. Respond to the prompt.

Imagine a big storm hit the area you live. **Design** a flyer for a donation event. Give details about the event. Tell people what they can donate. **Draw** a picture that helps people learn about the event.

Name: _____ Date: _____

Directions: Reread "Radio Weather Report." Respond to the prompt.

Imagine you live in the area where the hurricane hit. You listen to the radio weather report. You call the radio station to talk about your experience. **Write** answers to the questions. Tell what happened and how you felt.

Hello listener! What is your name?

_____

— — — — — — — — — — — — — — — — — — —

_____

Tell us about your hurricane experience.

_____

— — — — — — — — — — — — — — — — — — —

_____

_____

— — — — — — — — — — — — — — — — — — —

_____

_____

— — — — — — — — — — — — — — — — — — —

_____

What are you doing to stay calm?

_____

— — — — — — — — — — — — — — — — — — —

_____

_____

— — — — — — — — — — — — — — — — — — —

_____

Name: _____ Date: _____

Directions: Read the text. Answer the questions.

As You Read ⟩ Underline words that describe libraries.

A Trip to the Library

Libraries are all over the place! Some of them are small. Some of them are big. They can have thousands of books. They also have movies. People can borrow books from libraries. But first, they have to get library cards.

1. What do you need in order to borrow books from a library?
   - (A) a book to trade
   - (B) a library card
   - (C) five dollars

2. Which sentence is false?
   - (A) Libraries are all over.
   - (B) Libraries can be big and small.
   - (C) Libraries only have books.

3. What does it mean to *borrow books* from a library?
   - (A) take books to keep at home
   - (B) take books to read and then return them
   - (C) take books to read and then give to a friend

Name: _____ Date: _____

Directions: Read the text. Answer the questions.

> **As You Read** > Underline things you can do at the library.

A Special Place

Libraries have more than just books. Many of them have computers. They have places to sit and read. Some of them have story time for kids. Some of them have art classes.

Librarians work at libraries. They help people find what they need. They know a lot about research. And they know a lot about books. They want you to leave happy!

1. What is the main idea of this text?

    (A) The library has computers.

    (B) The library has more than just books.

    (C) Librarians know a lot about books.

2. Which word means more than one library?

    (A) librarians   (B) libraries   (C) librarian

3. Draw lines to match the pictures to the words.

computer

story time

art class

Name: _____ Date: _____

Directions: Read the text. Answer the questions.

> **As You Read** ⟩ Underline rules at libraries.

Library Rules

Anyone can use a library. But they have to follow the rules. People can take books home. But they have to return them. This is so other people have the chance to borrow books. If you damage a book, you have to pay a fine. Finally, be respectful. Libraries are very quiet. This helps people read.

1. What should you do if you take books home from the library?

- (A) Return them by the due date.
- (B) Keep them past the due date.
- (C) Not return the books.

2. Which word begins with the same sound as *whisper*?

- (A) borrow
- (B) worry
- (C) when

3. Why should you take books back to a library?

_____

_____

_____

_____

Name: _____ Date: _____

As You Read
Underline words that describe tiny libraries.
Circle who the books are for.

Tiny Libraries

Some libraries are very small. They are known as tiny libraries! You might see them in your neighborhood. On the outside, they look like dollhouses. On the inside, they have free books!

There are books for both kids and adults. People can take a book if they want to read it. Or, they can leave a book for someone else. Best of all, anyone can start a tiny library! All you need is a wooden box. It's a nice way to share books with others!

Directions: Read "Tiny Libraries." Answer the questions.

1. What is the purpose of tiny libraries?

   (A) for children to borrow books

   (B) for adults to trade books

   (C) for people to borrow and trade books

2. What should you do if you take a book from a tiny library?

   (A) You will need to bring the book back by the due date.

   (B) You can take a book and keep it at home.

   (C) You have to leave a book if you take one.

3. Which words are a pair of compound words?

   (A) neighborhood, dollhouse

   (B) someone, wooden

   (C) adults, inside

4. Trace the words. Write three facts about tiny libraries.

	Tiny Libraries
1.	
2.	
3.	

Name: _____ Date: _____

Directions: Reread "Tiny Libraries." Respond to the prompt.

Think about what you have learned about tiny libraries. What do they look like? How do they work? **Design** a tiny library. **Draw** a picture of it. **Write** the rules for your tiny library.

_____

_ _

_____

_ _

_____

Name: _____ Date: _____

Directions: Read the text. Answer the questions.

As You Read > Underline where the Book Club meets.

The Book Club

It was Tuesday night. The library had just closed. A group of books sat in a circle. They met every week for a few hours. They talked about the kids who had borrowed them. They talked about places they saw. They enjoyed sharing their stories with one another. They called it the *Book Club*.

1. When does the story take place?
   - (A) at a library
   - (B) Tuesday night
   - (C) in a circle

2. What makes this a fictional text?
   - (A) Books are acting like people.
   - (B) Book clubs are real.
   - (C) Kids are borrowing books.

3. What is the base word of *sharing*?
   - (A) shares
   - (B) share
   - (C) shared

Directions: Read the text. Answer the questions.

As You Read ⟩ Underline things that happened to the books.

Sharing Stories

"It's time for Book Club!" yelled a mystery book. The books formed a circle.

"I went to the beach," said a chapter book. "I got sand in all of my pages."

"That's nothing. Last week a little boy tore out some of my pages!" a mystery book cried out. The other books gasped in horror.

1. What is the purpose of the book club?

   Ⓐ The books talk about the librarians.

   Ⓑ The books tell stories to each other.

   Ⓒ The books clean the library.

2. What kind of stories do the two books share?

   Ⓐ They are both unpleasant.

   Ⓑ One is happy and one is sad.

   Ⓒ Both stories have happy endings.

3. What does the word *gasped* mean in this text?

   Ⓐ to yell very loud

   Ⓑ to take a sudden, fast breath

   Ⓒ to be scared

Directions: Read the text. Answer the questions.

As You Read 〉 Underline what the librarian asks.

Keeping a Secret

The library lights turned on. The books froze.

"Is someone here?" asked the librarian.

"We should just invite her," one book whispered.

"No! No one can know!" said another.

The librarian shrugged. She turned off the lights.

"Goodnight books," she said.

"She knows!" the books all whispered.

1. What is the librarian doing?
   (A) She is closing the library.
   (B) She is coming to join the book club.
   (C) She is opening the library.

2. Which word starts with the same sound as *knows*?
   (A) snore   (B) keep   (C) knock

3. Why do the books think the librarian knows about them?

   _____

   _

   _____

Name: _____ Date: _____

As You Read ⟩ Underline things the librarian does at Reading Club.

The Reading Club

The next day, the librarian hung up a sign. It said, "Reading Club! Wednesday nights at 7:00 p.m. All books are welcome."

"If you are going to have a book club, you should at least learn to read!" the librarian told the books. Each week, she read books out loud. She taught the books how to read. Sometimes, she read from one of the books in the group.

"We like this club much better! Thank you!" a book said.

"Yeah, now I actually know what I'm about!" said another book. Everyone laughed.

Directions: Read "The Reading Club." Answer the questions.

1. Why does the librarian put up a sign?

(A) to invite the books to the book club

(B) to tell the books to stop talking

(C) to invite children to come read the books

2. Why does the author call this text "The Reading Club"?

(A) The books don't want to learn how to read.

(B) The books are being read by the librarian.

(C) The books are learning how to read.

3. What is the base word of *yelled*?

(A) yells   (B) yell   (C) yelling

4. Write 1, 2, 3, or 4 to put the events in the correct order.

	The librarian tells them about the types of book clubs.
	The books show up to the reading club.
	The librarian hangs up a sign.
	The books tell the librarian "thank you."

Name: _____ Date: _____

Directions: Reread "The Reading Club." Respond to the prompt.

Imagine that you are starting a club. **Design** a poster for the club. **Write** details about the club and how people can join. Tell where and when the club will meet. **Draw** pictures to help share the details.

Name: _____ Date: _____

Read Me!

Hello, I'm a tiny library!

You can take a book from my shelf, and you don't have to bring it back.

I have one request. If you have an extra book at home, could you leave it here with me?

You could leave a book you think others will like.

I want to help people share their love of reading!

Thank you!

Name: _____ Date: _____

Directions: Read "Read Me!" Answer the questions.

1. Who is the narrator?
   - (A) a librarian
   - (B) a book
   - (C) a tiny library

2. What does the tiny library ask people to do?
   - (A) leave an extra book if they have one
   - (B) bring the books back
   - (C) don't take the books

3. Which word is spelled correctly?
   - (A) thier
   - (B) their
   - (C) theire

4. Where could this text be used? Why?

   _____

   _

   _____

   _

   _____

   _

   _____

   _

   _____

Directions: Read these texts. Look for ways the clubs in each text are the same and different. Write them in the chart.

Close-Reading Texts

Sharing Stories	The Reading Club
The books formed a circle. "I went to the beach," said a chapter book. "I got sand in all of my pages." "That's nothing. Last week a little boy tore out some of my pages!" a book cried out. The other books gasped in horror.	Each week, she read books out loud. She taught the books how to read. Sometimes, she read from one of the books in the group. "We like this club much better! Thank you!" a book said. "Yeah, now I actually know what I'm about!" said another book. Everyone laughed.

Comparing Book Clubs	
Alike	**Different**

Name: _____ Date: _____

Directions: Read the text. Reread "Read Me!" Write four things a library offers that a tiny library does not.

Close-Reading Text

A Special Place

Libraries have more than just books. Many of them have computers. They have places to sit and read. Some of them have story time for kids. Some of them have art classes.

Librarians work at libraries. They help people find what they need. They know a lot about research. And they know a lot about books. They want you to leave happy!

1. _____

2. _____

3. _____

4. _____

Name: _____ Date: _____

Directions: Think about the texts from this unit.
Respond to the prompt.

Write your own story about what books do after the
library closes at night. **Draw** a picture. **Share** your
story with a friend or adult.

_____
- -
_____
- -
_____
- -
_____
- -

_____
- - - - - - - - - - - - - - - - -
_____
- - - - - - - - - - - - - - - - -
_____
- - - - - - - - - - - - - - - - -
_____

Name: _____ Date: _____

Directions: Reread "Read Me!" Respond to the prompt.

Imagine that you have your own tiny library. **Write** a note from your tiny library. Tell people what you think it would want them to know. Your tiny library can have different rules from the one in this unit.

_____

_ _

_____

_ _

_____

_ _

_____

_ _

_____

_ _

_____

_ _

_____

_ _ _ _ _ _ _ _ _ _ _

_____

_ _ _ _ _ _ _ _ _ _ _

Name: _____ Date: _____

Directions: Read the text. Answer the questions.

As You Read › Underline the names of fruits.

Fruits and Seeds

Most fruits have seeds. Apples and oranges have seeds. Pumpkins do, too! The seeds from these fruits can be planted. They can grow more fruits.

Sometimes, farmers grow fruits without seeds. Some grapes are grown in a special way so they do not have seeds.

1. Why are seeds important?
   - (A) They are inside some fruits.
   - (B) They shouldn't be eaten.
   - (C) They can be planted to grow into more plants.

2. Why might farmers grow fruits without seeds?
   - (A) So that the birds won't eat the fruit.
   - (B) People want to eat fruit without the seeds.
   - (C) People like fruit.

3. Which word begins with the same sounds as *planted*?

   (A)    (B)   (C)

Name: _____ Date: _____

Directions: Read the text. Answer the questions.

As You Read Underline facts about apples.

Apple Trees

Apples grow on trees. Apples can be picked in the fall.

Apples come in many colors. They can be red, pink, green, or yellow.

People like to eat apples. People bake them into pies. Some people plant apple seeds. They want to grow more apple trees.

1. Which is another good title for this text?
   - (A) "Apples are Red"
   - (B) "All About Apples"
   - (C) "People Make Apple Pies!"

2. During which season are apples picked?
   - (A) fall
   - (B) winter
   - (C) spring

3. What does *replant* mean?
   - (A) pick
   - (B) plant for the first time
   - (C) plant again

Name: _____ Date: _____

Directions: Read the text. Answer the questions.

> **As You Read** > Underline what tomatoes are used for.

All About Tomatoes

Tomatoes need lots of sun to grow. They grow best when it is warm.

Tomatoes have seeds. That makes them a fruit. Eating them is good for your heart and skin.

Most tomatoes are sweet. They are used to make tomato sauce. They are used in salads and sandwiches, too.

1. What makes tomatoes fruits?

Ⓐ They have seeds.

Ⓑ They are good for your heart.

Ⓒ They need sun to grow.

2. Which word is spelled correctly?

Ⓐ tomatoe   Ⓑ tomatos   Ⓒ tomatoes

3. What did you learn about tomatoes from this text?

_____

_ _

_____

_ _

_____

Name: _____ Date: _____

As You Read ⟩ Underline a fact that is new or interesting. Circle action words that tell what people do with pumpkins.

Pumpkin Picking

Pumpkins can be picked in the fall. They start out green. They change color as they grow. They may turn orange or other colors. People can buy them at pumpkin patches. People can buy them at stores or farms, too.

Pumpkins have many uses. People can put them outside their houses. Some people paint or carve them. Some people eat them.

Inside, pumpkins have many seeds. People can plant the seeds. The seeds will grow into more pumpkins. People can also bake the seeds and eat them!

Directions: Read "Pumpkin Picking." Answer the questions.

1. Which color are pumpkins when they first begin to grow?

   (A) green   (B) orange   (C) yellow

2. What is one reason why people grow pumpkins?

   (A) People decorate them for Christmas.

   (B) People eat the seeds.

   (C) People use them in salads.

3. Which is a compound word?

   (A) decorations

   (B) outside

   (C) pumpkins

4. Trace the word in the center. Write one fact about pumpkins in each box.

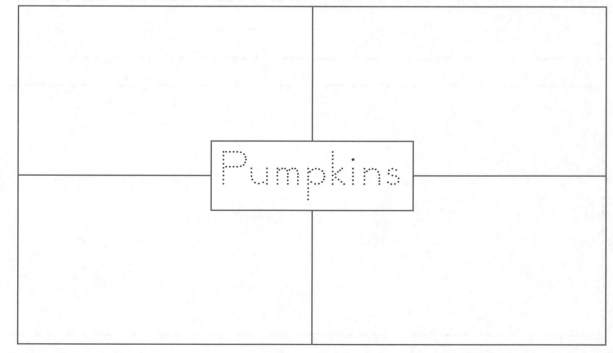

Name: _____ Date: _____

Directions: Reread "Pumpkin Picking." Respond to the prompt.

Write what you like to do with pumpkins. Do you carve them? Do you like to eat the seeds? Have you grown them? **Draw** a picture.

Name: _____ Date: _____

Directions: Read the text. Answer the questions.

> **As You Read** > Underline the question in the text.

A Pumpkin Surprise

"Mom, there's a pumpkin outside!" Harper yelled.

"That's not possible," Harper's mom said. "We haven't picked any."

Harper and her mom went to the front yard. They found a pumpkin. It looked just like the one they painted last year.

"How could this be here?" asked Harper's mom.

1. Who is narrating the text?

   (A) Harper   (B) a narrator   (C) Mom

2. What is the problem?

   (A) They like the pumpkin.

   (B) They are in the backyard.

   (C) They don't know where the pumpkin has come from.

3. Which words are in the correct alphabetical order?

   (A) mom, painted, pumpkin, thrown

   (B) painted, mom, pumpkin, thrown

   (C) mom, thrown, pumpkin, painted

Name: _____ Date: _____

Directions: Read the text. Answer the questions.

As You Read ⟩ Underline what Harper thinks the pumpkin is.

A Hungry Ghost

"I think it's a pumpkin ghost!" said Harper.

"You may be right!" said Harper's mom.

"I wonder why it came back," Harper said. "Maybe it knows that we give out the best Halloween candy!"

"Well, it's still a few days away," said her mom. "Maybe it will stick around."

1. Why does Harper call the pumpkin a *pumpkin ghost*?

   (A) It is very scary.

   (B) It has a sheet over it.

   (C) It comes back after they got rid of it.

2. What reason does Harper give for the pumpkin coming back?

   (A) It misses them.

   (B) It knows they give out the best candy.

   (C) It wants to be early for Halloween.

3. What does *stick around* mean in this text?

   (A) stay   (B) leave   (C) come back

Name: _____ Date: _____

Directions: Read the text. Answer the questions.

As You Read 〉 Underline the clue that tells
it is not Halloween day.

More Pumpkin Ghosts

The next night, there were 15 pumpkins
in the front yard.

"Mom!" Harper yelled. "Come look!"

"It looks like our old pumpkin invited
friends," Harper's mom said. "But they
are still too early for candy."

"I'm getting my camera." Harper said.

But when she came back, the
pumpkins had vanished.

1. Why does Harper's mom think there are more
   pumpkins?

   Ⓐ Their old pumpkin has invited its friends.

   Ⓑ They are from the neighbors' houses.

   Ⓒ The pumpkins grow there in the yard.

2. To which word has the suffix –*ing* been correctly
   added?

   Ⓐ geting   Ⓑ inviteing   Ⓒ getting

3. Retell what happened at the end of the text.

   _____

   _

   _____

Name: _____ Date: _____

Underline when Harper is speaking. Circle words that are about Halloween.

Giggling Ghosts

Harper told all her friends about the pumpkins.

"You're making this up," said her friend.

"I'm not! My mom sees them too!" Harper said.

To prove it, she invited her friends over on Halloween. But there were no pumpkins outside.

"Sorry. I guess they're not here," she said.

Then, Harper heard soft giggles. She looked up. The pumpkin ghosts were floating in her tree, smiling. Her friends gasped.

"It's Halloween night!" Harper yelled. "You can have your treats."

The pumpkin ghosts jumped down from the tree. They held out their buckets for candy. Harper and her friends laughed.

Directions: Read "Giggling Ghosts." Answer the questions.

1. Why does Harper invite her friends over on Halloween night?

  (A) to go trick-or-treating

  (B) to prove that there are ghost pumpkins

  (C) to carve pumpkins

2. Why are Harper and her friends not scared of the pumpkins?

  (A) The pumpkins are giggling and smiling.

  (B) The pumpkins are up in a tree.

  (C) The pumpkins disappear.

3. Which is the correct spelling of the word that means *also*?

  (A) to   (B) two   (C) too

4. Describe the beginning, middle, and end of the story.

Beginning	Middle	End

Name: _____ Date: _____

Directions: Reread "Giggling Ghosts." Respond to the prompt.

Imagine that you are one of Harper's friends at her house. **Write** about what you see. Tell what happens. **Draw** a picture.

_____

_____

_____

_____

_____

_____

_____

_____

Name: _____ Date: _____

Oops, I Ate a Seed

1

Oops, I swallowed a pumpkin seed.
Mom, am I going to turn into a pumpkin?

2

No, those are safe to eat.

Oh man, too bad. I was looking forward to a year-long costume.

3

What about a watermelon seed?

No, those are fine to eat too.

4

Hmm, do you know any good magicians that could help me?

Name: _____ **Date:** _____

Directions: Read "Oops, I Ate a Seed." Answer the questions.

1. What does the boy mean when he says he wants a *year-long costume*?

   Ⓐ He wishes it was Halloween all year.

   Ⓑ He wants his mom to buy him a Halloween costume.

   Ⓒ He wants to turn into a pumpkin or watermelon.

2. Why does the boy ask if his mom knows any good magicians?

   Ⓐ He wants the magician to turn him into a pumpkin or watermelon.

   Ⓑ He wants to pull a rabbit from a hat.

   Ⓒ He wants to scare his mother.

3. In which sentence does *swallowed* belong?

   Ⓐ He is _____ a seed.

   Ⓑ He _____ a seed.

   Ⓒ He will _____ a seed.

4. If you could wear a year-long costume, what would it be? Why?

_____

_____

_____

_____

Name: _____ Date: _____

Directions: Read these texts. Answer the questions on the chart.

Close-Reading Texts

Apple Trees	Pumpkin Picking
Apples grow on trees. Apples can be picked in the fall. Apples come in many colors. They can be red, pink, green, or yellow. People like to eat apples. Many people bake them into apple pies.	Pumpkins can be picked in the fall. They start out green. They change color as they grow. They may turn orange or other colors. People can buy them at pumpkin patches. People can buy them at stores or farms, too. Pumpkins have many uses. People can put them outside their houses. Some people paint or carve them. Some people eat them.

Questions	Apple Trees	Pumpkin Picking
When is the fruit picked?		
What colors can the fruit be?		
What can you do with the fruit?		

Name: _____ Date: _____

Directions: Read the text. Then, reread "Oops, I Ate a Seed." Write ways the texts are similar. Write ways the texts are different.

Close-Reading Text

Giggling Ghosts
"Sorry. I guess they're not here," she said.
Then, Harper heard soft giggles. She looked up. The pumpkin ghosts were floating in her tree, smiling. Her friends gasped.
"It's Halloween night!" Harper yelled. "You can have your treats."
The pumpkin ghosts jumped down from the tree. They held out their buckets for candy. Harper and her friends laughed.

Similarities

1. _____

2. _____

Differences

1. _____

2. _____

Name: _____ Date: _____

Directions: Think about the texts from this unit. Respond to the prompt.

Choose a fruit from this unit that you like. Pretend you are the fruit. **Write** some facts about the fruit. **Draw** a picture.

_____

- - - - - - - - - - - - - - - - -

I Am a _____

- -

_____

- -

_____

- -

_____

- - - - - - - - - - - - - - - -

_____

- - - - - - - - - - - - - - - -

_____

- - - - - - - - - - - - - - - -

_____

- - - - - - - - - - - - - - - -

_____

Name: _____ Date: _____

Directions: Reread "Oops, I Ate A Seed." Respond to the prompt.

Add two frames to the story. How will his mother answer him? Will he ask about other seeds? Will he say something silly? **Draw** pictures. **Write** what the characters say.

Hmm, do you know any good magicians that could help me?

Name: _____ Date: _____

Directions: Read the text. Answer the questions.

As You Read ⟩ Underline the ship captains' goal.

Treasure!

Long ago, some ship captains had one goal. They wanted to steal all the gold they could. Some kings and queens asked the captains to steal. They were expected to share the treasures.

1. What goal did the ship captains have?
   - (A) catch pirates
   - (B) steal gold
   - (C) become kings

2. What did some kings and queens want?
   - (A) to get some of the stolen treasure
   - (B) to learn about the seas
   - (C) to have captains fight for them

3. Who does *they* refer to in this text?
   - (A) the captains
   - (B) kings and queens
   - (C) the treasure

Name: _____ Date: _____

Directions: Read the text. Answer the questions.

As You Read ⟩ Put a ☆ next to new or interesting facts.

The Most Famous Pirate

Edward Teach was a scary man. He had a long, black beard. He liked to have several pistols. He put knives in his belt. He captured many ships. Edward Teach was also known as Blackbeard. He was the most famous pirate!

1. Which is **not** true about Edward Teach?
   - (A) He was famous.
   - (B) He was Blackbeard.
   - (C) He was a king.

2. What is something Edward Teach did as a pirate?
   - (A) Become a king.
   - (B) Capture many ships.
   - (C) Build a ship.

3. The word Blackbeard is a compound word. It is made of two smaller words: *Black–beard*. Which word is also a compound word?
   - (A) biggest
   - (B) planter
   - (C) tablecloth

Name: _____ Date: _____

Directions: Read the text. Answer the questions.

As You Read > Underline facts about sloops.

A Pirate Ship

A sloop was one of the best ships pirates could use. It was not the biggest kind of ship. But it was fast. This helped pirates win battles. The pirates could attack and get away quickly.

1. Why was a sloop a good ship for a pirate?

   (A) It was one of the biggest ships.

   (B) It could never be caught.

   (C) It was fast during a pirate attack.

2. Which word has the same vowel sound as *sloop*?

   (A) book   (B) roof   (C) foot

3. What did you learn about pirate ships from this text?

   _____

   -

   _____

   -

   _____

Name: _____ Date: _____

As You Read Underline something that is new or interesting. Circle important words.

A Different Pirate

Mary Read was an unlucky woman. She lived long ago. It was hard for her to find work. So, she decided to fight in a war. She dressed like men did back then. Then, she got married. But her husband died. She wanted to sail away. But pirates attacked her ship. Mary chose to stay with them. She became a pirate. Later, the group of pirates got caught. Mary went to jail.

Mary Read

Name: _____ Date: _____

Directions: Read "A Different Pirate." Answer the questions.

1. Which sentence is true?
   - (A) Only men were pirates.
   - (B) Only women were pirates.
   - (C) Men and women were pirates.

2. Why did Mary dress like a man?
   - (A) so she could sail on a ship
   - (B) so she could fight in a war
   - (C) so she could get married

3. Why do you think Mary was put in jail?
   - (A) Mary was poor and stole bread.
   - (B) Mary wanted to sail away.
   - (C) Mary was a pirate who stole things.

4. Trace the words. Write three events in Mary Read's life. Write them in the correct order.

Mary Read

Event 1	
Event 2	
Event 3	

Name: _____ Date: _____

Directions: Reread "A Different Pirate." Respond to the prompt.

Imagine you are a pirate. **Write** about a day in your life as a pirate. **Draw** a picture.

_____

- -

_____

- -

_____

- -

_____

- -

_____

Name: _____ Date: _____

Directions: Read the text. Answer the questions.

> **As You Read** Underline what was in the bottle.

A Buried Bottle

Cole was in his backyard one day. His parents were getting a pool. There was a big pile of dirt on the ground. Cole was digging in the dirt when he spotted an old bottle. He opened it up. There was an old treasure map inside!

1. Why is there a pile of dirt?
   - Ⓐ They are putting new plants in the backyard.
   - Ⓑ They made a pile for Cole to play in.
   - Ⓒ They are digging a hole for a pool.

2. What is the setting of this story?
   - Ⓐ in Cole's house
   - Ⓑ the backyard
   - Ⓒ the swimming pool

3. Which word describes the bottle?
   - Ⓐ old
   - Ⓑ new
   - Ⓒ broken

Name: _____ Date: _____

Directions: Read the text. Answer the questions.

> **As You Read** Underline what the map looks like.

Buried Treasure

Cole showed the treasure map to all his friends.

"It looks like a pirate's map. Maybe it's for buried treasure!" Theo said.

"We should follow it," Cole said.

"Did pirates really bury treasure? Or is that just made up?" another friend asked.

"I guess we'll find out," Cole said.

1. Who does Cole show the map to?

   (A) his parents   (B) his friends   (C) Theo

2. What does it mean when Cole says, "I guess we'll find out"?

   (A) They think the treasure is made up.

   (B) They will show the map to Cole's parents.

   (C) They will follow the treasure map.

3. What is the base word of *buried*?

   (A) bury   (B) berry   (C) buriesback

Name: _____ Date: _____

Directions: Read the text. Answer the questions.

As You Read ⟩ Underline things Cole and his friends do.

A Birthday Trick

Cole and his friends followed the clues on the map. It led to the park! They found where the treasure was buried. They started digging. They found a small chest filled with fake coins.

"This isn't real money," Cole said.

"No, but you can all use them at the arcade! Happy early birthday!" his parents shouted. Cole smiled ear to ear.

1. How do you know that it is not Cole's exact birthday?
   - (A) They are not at the arcade.
   - (B) The treasure is not buried in his backyard.
   - (C) His parents say "Happy early birthday!"

2. What does the phrase *smiled ear to ear* mean?
   - (A) Cole was not smiling.
   - (B) Cole had a big smile.
   - (C) Cole's ears hurt.

3. Why were Cole's parents at the park?

   _____

   _ _ _ _ _ _ _ _ _ _ _ _ _ _ _ _ _ _ _

   _____

Arcade Treasure

The chest had 300 coins! Cole started handing them out to his friends. They were so excited. Cole still couldn't believe it. He was so happy his parents had surprised them.

Cole and his friends went to the arcade. They played for hours. They gathered all their tickets together in the end. They had enough for a model! They went back to Cole's house to build it. It was a pirate ship!

Directions: Read "Arcade Treasure." Answer the questions.

1. What do Cole and his friends do with their tickets?
   (A) They save them.
   (B) They give them away.
   (C) They combine them.

2. How many coins does the chest have?
   (A) three hundred
   (B) thirty hundred
   (C) three thousand

3. What is an *arcade*?
   (A) a place to watch movies
   (B) a place to play games
   (C) a place where kids go to swim

4. Write 1, 2, 3, 4, or 5 next to each sentence to retell the story in the correct order.

	They played for hours.
	Cole handed out the coins to his friends.
	Cole and his friends built a pirate ship model.
	They went to the arcade.
	They gathered all their tickets together.

Name: _____ Date: _____

Directions: Reread "Arcade Treasure." Respond to the prompt.

Imagine you want to throw a surprise birthday party for someone. **Write** a plan for the surprise. Tell who you would surprise and how. **Draw** a picture.

_____

_ _

_____

_____

_ _

_____

_____

_ _

_____

Name: _____ Date: _____

Dear Diary

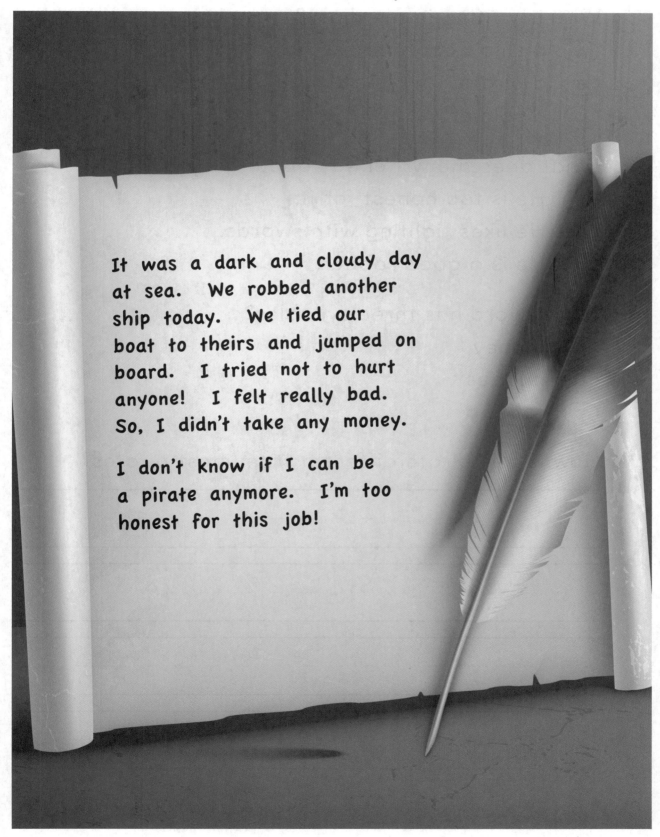

It was a dark and cloudy day at sea. We robbed another ship today. We tied our boat to theirs and jumped on board. I tried not to hurt anyone! I felt really bad. So, I didn't take any money.

I don't know if I can be a pirate anymore. I'm too honest for this job!

Name: _____ Date: _____

Directions: Read "Dear Diary." Answer the questions.

1. Who is writing in the diary?
   - (A) a ship's captain
   - (B) a pirate
   - (C) a soldier

2. What does the writer say about his job?
   - (A) He is too honest for it.
   - (B) He likes fighting with swords.
   - (C) He is a good robber.

3. Which word has three syllables?
   - (A) money
   - (B) injuries
   - (C) robbed

4. How is this pirate different from most pirates?
   _____
   _____
   _____
   _____
   _____
   _____

Name: _____ Date: _____

Directions: Read these texts. Write the cause or effect for each text.

Close-Reading Texts

Buried Treasure

Cole showed the treasure map to all his friends.

"It looks like a pirate's map. Maybe it's for buried treasure!" Theo said.

"We should follow it," Cole said.

"Did pirates really bury treasure? Or is that just made up?" another friend asked.

"I guess we'll find out," Cole said.

Cause

Cole showed the treasure map to all his friends.

Effect

A Birthday Trick

They found where the treasure was buried. They started digging. They found a small chest filled with fake coins.

"This isn't real money," Cole said.

"No, but you can all use them at the arcade! Happy early birthday!" his parents shouted. Cole smiled ear to ear.

Cause

Effect

Cole smiled ear to ear.

Name: _____ Date: _____

Directions: Read these texts. Answer the questions.

Close-Reading Texts

A Different Pirate	Dear Diary
Mary Read was an unlucky woman. She lived long ago. It was hard for her to find work. So, she decided to fight in a war. She dressed like men did back then. Then, she got married. But her husband died. She wanted to sail away. But pirates attacked her ship. Mary chose to stay with them. She became a pirate. Later, the group of pirates got caught. Mary went to jail.	It was a dark and cloudy day at sea. We robbed another ship today. We tied our boat to theirs and jumped on board. I tried not to hurt anyone! I felt really bad. So, I didn't take any money. I don't know if I can be a pirate anymore. I'm too honest for this job!

Questions	A Different Pirate	Dear Diary
Who is the main character or person?		
Do they want to be a pirate?		

135043—180 Days of Reading   © Shell Education

Name: _____ Date: _____

Directions: Think about the texts from this unit.
Respond to the prompt.

Sailors often sang songs called *sea shanties* as they
worked. **Imagine** you are a pirate. Fill in the blanks
to complete the sea shanty. It is about your buried
treasure. **Draw** a picture.

A Pirate's Life for Me

_____

I'm a _____ on the sea.

It's a _____ life for me!

The treasure chest is full of _____.

I hope I can find it when I come _____.

Name: _____ Date: _____

Directions: Reread "Dear Diary." Respond to the prompt.

> **Imagine** you are the pirate that wrote in the diary. **Write** a new page in your diary. **Write** what you would like to do and be instead of a pirate. **Draw** a picture.

Dear Diary,

_____

- -

_____

- -

_____

- -

_____

- - - - - - - - - - - - - - -

_____

- - - - - - - - - - - - - - -

_____

- - - - - - - - - - - - - - -

_____

Name: _____ Date: _____

Directions: Read the text. Answer the questions.

As You Read 〉 Underline words that describe the insect.

A Large Insect

You may see lots of insects this summer. But you will not find these bugs in your yard. They are called hissing cockroaches. They live on a large island near Africa. Each one is two to three inches (five to eight centimeters) long. Each one is as wide as a paper clip.

1. What do you know about this cockroach?
   - (A) It lives on an island.
   - (B) You can find it in your yard.
   - (C) It is only found in the summer.

2. What can be said about its size?
   - (A) It is smaller than many insects.
   - (B) It is bigger than many insects.
   - (C) It is the largest insect.

3. What is an island?
   - (A) a river near an ocean
   - (B) a tall mountain
   - (C) land with water all around it

Name: _____ Date: _____

Directions: Read the text. Answer the questions.

> **As You Read** Underline what the cockroaches eat.

Cockroach Lives

Hissing cockroaches hide on forest floors. They come out at night. They start looking for fruit or plants to eat.

male

Male and female hissing cockroaches look different. The males have horns on their heads. The females have bumps. And, they are both wingless. They are not pests.

female

1. When do these cockroaches come out to eat?

    (A) during the day

    (B) in the morning

    (C) at night

2. How can you tell a male hissing cockroach from a female?

    (A) by their color

    (B) by their heads

    (C) by their tails

3. What does *wingless* mean in this text?

    (A) with many wings

    (B) with one wing

    (C) without wings

Name: _____ Date: _____

Directions: Read the text. Answer the questions.

As You Read ⟩ Underline new or interesting facts.

Time to Fight

The male cockroaches like to fight. They ram their horns into each other. They also make noise. They hiss at each other. They push air out through breathing holes in their bodies. This noise explains how they got their name!

1. How do the males fight?

- Ⓐ ram and hiss
- Ⓑ punch and hit
- Ⓒ kick and spit

2. How did this type of cockroach get its name?

- Ⓐ what it eats
- Ⓑ a noise it makes
- Ⓒ how it looks

3. How do these cockroaches make noise?

_____

_____

_____

_____

Name: _____ Date: _____

As You Read ⟩ Underline a fact that is new or interesting. Share it with a friend or adult.

Raising Hissing Cockroaches

Some people raise hissing cockroaches. They keep them in dry fish tanks with lids. The glass allows people to look inside. The tanks need to have bedding. The tanks also need fresh water. And, the cockroaches also need food. It doesn't have to be special food. They can eat dog food. For a treat, they like apple slices.

Female cockroaches carry eggs inside their bodies. They can have 50 babies at a time. So if you raise cockroaches, you'll have a lot before you know it!

Directions: Read "Raising Hissing Cockroaches." Answer the questions.

1. Why would you need a lid on the dry fish tank?
   - (A) The cockroaches could fly out.
   - (B) The cockroaches could crawl out.
   - (C) The cockroaches could swim out.

2. What is the main idea?
   - (A) Cockroaches like to live in the forest.
   - (B) It is not hard to have a pet cockroach.
   - (C) Cockroaches are pests.

3. What does the word *bedding* mean in this text?
   - (A) something for the insects to live on
   - (B) some sheets and blankets
   - (C) something for the insects to eat

4. Trace the words. Write three facts about keeping hissing cockroaches as pets.

Hissing Cockroaches

1.	
2.	
3.	

Name: _____ Date: _____

Directions: Reread "Hissing Cockroaches." Respond to the prompt.

Imagine you have a hissing cockroach for a pet.
Write about your pet cockroach. What is its name?
Where did you get it? How do you take care of it?
Draw a picture.

_____

_____

_____

_____

_____

_____

_____

_____

Name: _____ Date: _____

Directions: Read the text. Answer the questions.

As You Read ⟩ Underline how the characters catch the butterflies.

Catching Butterflies

My brother and I love butterflies. We love their beautiful colors. We have nets to try to catch them in our backyard. We don't catch many. There aren't a lot near our home. Plus, they fly very fast!

1. Why don't they catch many butterflies?
   - (A) They have bad nets.
   - (B) They don't know how to catch them.
   - (C) There are not many near their home.

2. What do they enjoy about butterflies?
   - (A) their colors
   - (B) their noises
   - (C) their smell

3. What does the illustration show and help you understand?
   - (A) It shows how they chase butterflies.
   - (B) It shows that the narrator is a girl.
   - (C) It shows that the narrator is a boy.

Name: _____ Date: _____

Directions: Read the text. Answer the questions.

As You Read Underline things their mom tells them.

Colorful Flowers

We ask our mom how we can catch more butterflies. She says they like colorful flowers. She says she will take us to the plant store to buy some flowers. We can plant them in our yard. Soon, we should have more butterflies!

1. Who tells them how to attract more butterflies?

   Ⓐ the person at the plant store

   Ⓑ their mom

   Ⓒ a book

2. Why are they going to buy colorful flowers?

   Ⓐ Butterflies like colorful flowers.

   Ⓑ There are butterflies at the plant store.

   Ⓒ Their mom wants more flowers in their garden.

3. The word *colorful* means full of color. What does *beautiful* mean?

   Ⓐ full of butterflies

   Ⓑ full of blossoms

   Ⓒ full of beauty

Name: _____ Date: _____

Directions: Read the text. Answer the questions.

As You Read > Underline how the narrator feels about bees.

The Helper Bees

We plant brightly colored flowers. In a few days, we see some butterflies. Our plan worked! But we also see more bees. I'm scared of bees. My mom says not to worry. If we don't bother them, they won't bother us. She says that they help the flowers.

1. What does their mom say about bees?

   Ⓐ *If we don't bother them, they won't bother us.*

   Ⓑ *Our plan worked!*

   Ⓒ *I'm scared of bees.*

2. What does the word *won't* mean?

   Ⓐ will not

   Ⓑ was not

   Ⓒ won't not

3. What are the effects of the characters planting colorful flowers?

   _____

   _____

   _____

   _____

Name: _____ Date: _____

Growing the Garden

My brother and I watch the butterflies in our garden. We draw pictures of their beautiful wings. Sometimes, we chase them. Sometimes, we think they chase us! We even like the bees now, too. I ended up getting used to them. Next year, we are going to grow more flowers. We hope we have more bugs in our yard next summer!

Directions: Read "Growing the Garden." Answer the questions.

1. What do the children enjoy doing with the butterflies?

   (A) watching, drawing, and catching them

   (B) watching, drawing, and chasing them

   (C) watching, chasing, and catching them

2. When are they going to grow more flowers?

   (A) next year

   (B) next week

   (C) next weekend

3. Which word is a compound word?

   (A) garden   (B) beautiful   (C) sometimes

4. Complete the sentences to retell the story.

The brother and sister draw pictures of the butterfly's

_____

_____.

_____

_____

They even like the _____, now.

Next year, they want to grow more

_____

_____

_____.

They also hope to have more

_____

_____

_____ in their garden.

Name: _____ Date: _____

Directions: Reread "Growing the Garden." Respond to the prompt.

You get to design and plant a garden. **Write** about your garden. What kind of plants would you get? How would you decorate it? What would you want to do in your garden? **Draw** a picture of it.

_____

- -

_____

- -

_____

- -

_____

- -

_____

Name: _____ Date: _____

Watch Your Step!

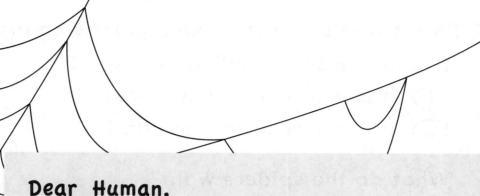

Dear Human,

Let's start by saying that we know you don't want us here.

But it's so warm inside. You have a lovely home.

We really appreciate you letting us live here for free.

We just have one small thing to ask: could you watch your step?

We're so little, and we can't talk.

We hope we can become good housemates to you one day.

If you let us stay, we'll be sure to eat those other bugs you don't like.

Sincerely,

Spiders in your house

Name: _____ Date: _____

Directions: Read "Watch Your Step!" Answer the questions.

1. What do the spiders like about living inside?
   - (A) it is warm, small, and free
   - (B) it is warm, lovely, and free
   - (C) it is warm, scary, and dark

2. What do the spiders want?
   - (A) for us to not step on them
   - (B) for us to welcome the other bugs
   - (C) for us to have a lovely home

3. What is an antonym for *here*?
   - (A) their
   - (B) there
   - (C) they're

4. How does this letter change your feelings about spiders in your house?

   _____

   _____

   _____

   _____

   _____

Name: _____ Date: _____

Directions: Read these texts. Answer the questions to show how the characters change.

Close-Reading Texts

Catching Butterflies	Growing the Garden
My brother and I love butterflies. We love their beautiful colors. We have nets to try to catch them in our backyard. We don't catch many. There aren't a lot near our home. Plus, they fly very fast!	My brother and I watch the butterflies in our garden. We draw pictures of their beautiful wings. Sometimes, we chase them. Sometimes, we think they chase us! We even like the bees now, too. I ended up getting used to them.

Questions	Catching Butterflies	Growing the Garden
How do they feel about butterflies?		
What do they do with butterflies?		

Name: _____ Date: _____

Directions: Read the text. Reread "Watch Your Step!" Write four ways the bugs in the two texts are different.

Close-Reading Text

Raising Hissing Cockroaches

Some people raise hissing cockroaches. They keep them in dry fish tanks with lids. The glass allows people to look inside. The tanks need to have bedding. The tanks also need fresh water. And, the cockroaches also need food. It doesn't have to be special food. They can eat dog food. For a treat, they like apple slices.

Female cockroaches carry eggs inside their bodies. They can have 50 babies at a time. So if you raise cockroaches, you'll have a lot before you know it!

_____

1. _____

2. _____

3. _____

4. _____

Name: _____ Date: _____

Directions: Reread "Watch Your Step!" Respond to the prompt.

Add to the spiders' letter. **Write** three more reasons why the humans should be nice to them. **Draw** a picture with each reason.

Name: _____ Date: _____

Directions: Reread "Watch Your Step!" Respond to the prompt.

Think about other bugs or animals that humans live near. **Write** a letter from a bug or animal to you. For example, what might a squirrel in the backyard say to you if they could write you a letter? What would they ask for? **Draw** a picture.

_____

_____

_____ ,

_____

_____

_____

_____

_____

_____

_____

_____ ,

_____

_____

Standards Correlations

Shell Education is committed to producing educational materials that are research and standards based. To support this effort, this resource is correlated to the academic standards of all 50 states, the District of Columbia, the Department of Defense Dependent Schools, and the Canadian provinces. A correlation is also provided for key professional educational organizations.

To print a customized correlation report for your state, visit our website at **www.tcmpub.com/administrators/correlations** and follow the online directions. If you require assistance in printing correlation reports, please contact the Customer Service Department at 1-800-858-7339.

Standards Overview

The Every Student Succeeds Act (ESSA) mandates that all states adopt challenging academic standards that help students meet the goal of college and career readiness. While many states already adopted academic standards prior to ESSA, the act continues to hold states accountable for detailed and comprehensive standards. Standards are designed to focus instruction and guide adoption of curricula. They define the knowledge, skills, and content students should acquire at each level. Standards are also used to develop standardized tests to evaluate students' academic progress. State standards are used in the development of our resources, so educators can be assured they meet state academic requirements.

College and Career Readiness

Today's college and career readiness (CCR) standards offer guidelines for preparing K–12 students with the knowledge and skills that are necessary to succeed in postsecondary job training and education. CCR standards include the Common Core State Standards as well as other state-adopted standards such as the Texas Essential Knowledge and Skills. The standards found on page 228 describe the content presented throughout the lessons.

TESOL and WIDA Standards

English language development standards are integrated within each lesson to enable English learners to work toward proficiency in English while learning content—developing the skills and confidence in listening, speaking, reading, and writing. The standards found in the digital resources describe the language objectives presented throughout the lessons.

Standards Correlations *(cont.)*

180 Days of Reading for First Grade, 2nd Edition offers a full page of daily reading comprehension and word analysis practice activities for each day of the school year.

Every first grade unit provides questions and activities tied to a wide variety of language arts standards, providing students opportunities for regular practice in reading comprehension, word recognition, and writing. The focus of the first two weeks in each unit alternates between nonfiction and fiction standards, with the third week focusing on both, as students read nontraditional texts and complete paired-text activities.

Reading Comprehension

Read and comprehend complex literary and informational texts independently and proficiently.

Read closely to determine what the text says explicitly. Ask and answer questions about the text and make logical inferences.

Determine central ideas or themes of a text and analyze their development; summarize the key supporting details and ideas.

Analyze how and why individuals, events, or ideas develop and interact over the course of a text.

Recognize and analyze genre-specific characteristics, structures, and purposes within and across diverse texts.

Use metacognitive skills to both develop and deepen comprehension of texts.

Analyze how two or more texts address similar themes or topics in order to build knowledge or to compare the approaches the authors take.

Assess how point of view or purpose shapes the content and style of texts.

Reading Foundational Skills

Know and apply grade-level phonics and word analysis skills in decoding words.

Language and Vocabulary Acquisition

Determine or clarify the meaning of unknown and multiple-meaning words and phrases by using context clues, analyzing meaningful word parts, and consulting general and specialized reference materials, as appropriate,

Demonstrate understanding of figurative language, word relationships, and nuances in word meanings.

Writing

Produce clear and coherent writing in which the development, organization, and style are appropriate to task, purpose, genre, and audience.

Respond to and draw evidence from literary or informational texts to show analysis, reflection, and research.

Writing Rubric

Score students' written response using the rubric below. Display the rubric for students to reference as they write. A student version of this rubric is provided in the digital resources.

Points	Criteria
4	• Uses an appropriate organizational sequence to produce very clear and coherent writing. • Uses descriptive language that develops or clarifies ideas. • Engages the reader. • Uses a style very appropriate to task, purpose, and audience.
3	• Uses an organizational sequence to produce clear and coherent writing. • Uses descriptive language that develops or clarifies ideas. • Engages the reader. • Uses a style appropriate to task, purpose, and audience.
2	• Uses an organizational sequence to produce somewhat clear and coherent writing. • Uses some descriptive language that develops or clarifies ideas. • Engages the reader in some way. • Uses a style somewhat appropriate to task, purpose, and audience.
1	• Does not use an organized sequence; the writing is not clear or coherent. • Uses little descriptive language to develop or clarify ideas. • Does not engage the reader. • Does not use a style appropriate to task, purpose, or audience.
0	• Offers no writing or does not respond to the assignment presented.

References Cited

Gough, Philip B., and William E. Tunmer. 1986. "Decoding, Reading, and Reading Disability." *Remedial and Special Education* 7 (1): 6–10.

Marzano, Robert. 2010. "When Practice Makes Perfect...Sense." *Educational Leadership* 68 (3): 81–83.

National Reading Panel. 2000. *Report of the National Reading Panel: Teaching Children to Read. Report of the Subgroups.* Washington, D.C.: U.S. Department of Health and Human Services, National Institutes of Health.

Scarborough, Hollis S. 2001. "Connecting Early Language and Literacy to Later Reading (Dis)abilities: Evidence, Theory, and Practice." In *Handbook of Early Literacy Research*, edited by Susan B. Neuman and David K. Dickinson, 97–110. New York: Guilford.

Soalt, Jennifer. 2005. "Bringing Together Fictional and Informational Texts to Improve Comprehension." *The Reading Teacher* 58 (7): 680–683.

Answer Key

Unit 1

Week 1

Day 1 (page 11)
1. B
2. A
3. B

Day 2 (page 12)
1. B
2. C
3. B

Day 3 (page 13)
1. A
2. C
3. Answers should include an illustration of the main idea, such as cows eating grass, with labeled parts.

Day 4 (page 15)
1. C
2. A
3. C
4. Answers should include three details about dinosaur teeth.

Day 5 (page 16)
Answers should describe a new kind of dinosaur, its teeth, and what it ate, and include a picture.

Week 2

Day 1 (page 17)
1. B
2. C
3. A

Day 2 (page 18)
1. A
2. A
3. B

Day 3 (page 19)
1. A
2. C
3. Answers should describe whether it would be less scary to be a tooth fairy for bunnies and why.

Day 4 (page 21)
1. B
2. C
3. B
4. Answers should include 4 words or phrases that describe the problems the tooth fairy is having.

Day 5 (page 22)
Answers should include a letter from the tooth fairy to a pizza company telling why the fairy wants to deliver pizza and will be good at it.

Week 3

Day 1 (page 24)
1. C
2. A
3. B
4. Answers should describe why someone would want to find shark teeth for the foundation, such as for the money.

Day 2 (page 25)
Example

About the Text	Dinosaur Teeth	Shark Teeth Wanted
Purpose of the Text	to inform readers about dinosaur teeth	to get people to find and send in shark teeth
One Key Detail	some had no teeth	$20 reward
Important Words About the Topic	diplodocus, chew, swallowed, pointed, spoons	losing, studying, health, sharks, teeth, reward

Day 2 (page 25)
Example

The Dinosaur Dentist	Tooth Fairy Troubles
see teeth	dangerous
bring teeth to the dinosaur dentist	could get bit or eaten
	needs helpers

Day 4 (page 27)
Answers should include pictures of what the fairy might dream about and sentences about the dream.

Day 5 (page 28)
Answers should include a picture of shark teeth and a letter telling the biologists about the teeth they are sending with questions about the shark teeth.

Unit 2

Week 1

Day 1 (page 29)
1. C
2. B
3. A

Answer Key (cont.)

Day 2 (page 30)
1. B
2. C
3. A

Day 3 (page 31)
1. A
2. C
3. Answers should include a description of where the student feels warm and safe like a bear in a den.

Day 4 (page 33)
1. A
2. B
3. C
4. Answers should include two important facts about bear hibernation.

Day 5 (page 34)
Answers should describe what they think bears feel like when they wake up in the spring and include a picture.

Week 2

Day 1 (page 35)
1. C
2. B
3. C

Day 2 (page 36)
1. B
2. A
3. B

Day 3 (page 37)
1. A
2. C
3. Answers should describe how turtles and bears are alike, such as the fact that they both hibernate.

Day 4 (page 39)
1. B
2. A
3. A
4. 3, 1, 2.

Day 5 (page 40)
Answer should describe a turtle that is looking for a place to sleep all winter and include a picture.

Week 3

Day 1 (page 42)
1. C
2. B
3. B
4. Answers should include that the groundhog finds a place to hibernate under the shed.

Day 2 (page 43)
Answers should include two facts or statements about hibernation from each text.

Day 3 (page 44)
Answers should include one way the texts are similar, such as both being about animals that hibernate, and one way they are different, such as one being fiction and one being nonfiction.

Day 4 (page 45)
Answers should include six important words about hibernation from the texts to make a poem using the frame provided.

Day 5 (page 46)
Answer should describe hibernating from Tork's point of view. Student should draw a picture of Tork hibernating with a "Do Not Disturb" sign.

Unit 3

Week 1

Day 1 (page 47)
1. C
2. B
3. A

Day 2 (page 48)
1. C
2. B
3. C

Day 3 (page 49)
1. B
2. C
3. Answers should include that Mr. Poppen added a rope so the skis could be controlled.

Day 4 (page 51)
1. A
2. A
3. B
4. last, then, first

Day 5 (page 52)
Answers should describe how students would make a toy that combines skiing with a sport other than surfing. Students should draw and label pictures of the new toy.

Week 2

Day 1 (page 53)
1. B
2. A
3. C

Day 2 (page 54)
1. A
2. B
3. C

Answer Key (cont.)

Day 3 (page 55)

1. A
2. B
3. Answers should tell that Zoe says, "Time for school!" which shows she is excited. The exclamation mark shows that she is saying it with excitement.

Day 4 (page 57)

1. C
2. A
3. A
4. Answers should include three things that Zoe and Taj do at ski school, such as learning how to get up, riding the ski lift, and zipping down the hill.

Day 5 (page 58)

Answers should include how Zoe and Taj's day might be if they did not have a ski lesson and should include an illustration of the new story.

Week 3

Day 1 (page 60)

1. B
2. C
3. B
4. Answers should include a designed flyer with pictures for the play "Goldilocks an the Three Bears," what the show is about, and why people should come.

Day 2 (page 61)

Answers should include circled words about skiing from each text and setences using three of the words.

Day 3 (page 62)

Answers should describe what the texts are mostly about, such as how the snurfer came to be developed and what the ski lessons include.

Day 4 (page 63)

Answers should include a letter to a friend about ski school to persuade the friend to come. Each student should also draw a picture.

Day 5 (page 64)

Answers should include a designed flyer with pictures for the play "Goldilocks and the Three Bears" with details about what it is all about.

Unit 4

Week 1

Day 1 (page 65)

1. A
2. B
3. B

Day 2 (page 66)

1. B
2. A
3. C

Day 3 (page 67)

1. B
2. A
3. A customer doesn't like his potatoes, so Mr. Crim cuts them extra thin and fries them crisp.

Day 4 (page 69)

1. C
2. B
3. B
4. Answers should include two facts about crisps.

Day 5 (page 70)

Answers should include an advertisement with a picture for Mr. Crum's restaurant and crisps.

Week 2

Day 1 (page 71)

1. B
2. A
3. A

Day 2 (page 72)

1. B
2. C
3. B

Day 3 (page 73)

1. C
2. B
3. Answers should include evidence that Erin is having a good day, such as eating chips that taste great and making some new friends.

Day 4 (page 75)

1. C
2. B
3. A
4. Answers should describe the beginning, middle, and end of the text.

Day 5 (page 76)

Answers should describe Erin's last day of testing from her point of view. Students should also draw a picture.

Week 3

Day 1 (page 78)

1. C
2. A
3. B
4. Answers should describe which parts of the potato chip recipe they think would be hard to do.

Day 2 (page 79)

Answers should describe one way that characters or things change in each text, such as Mr. Crum getting his own restaurant and Erin making friends.

Answer Key *(cont.)*

Day 3 (page 80)

Example

Text	Words About Chips
Crisp Potatoes	sliced, thin, fried, crisp
Potato Chip Recipe	slice, thin, golden brown

Day 4 (page 81)

Answers should include an article for a newspaper as a food writer. Students should critique Mr. Crum's crisps and draw a picture.

Day 5 (page 82)

Answers should include a recipe for a food the student enjoys and a picture of it.

Unit 5

Week 1

Day 1 (page 83)

1. C
2. A
3. A

Day 2 (page 84)

1. B
2. A
3. B

Day 3 (page 85)

1. C
2. B
4. Answers should include the main idea that firetrucks are built to help.

Day 4 (page 87)

1. B
2. C
3. C
4. Answers should include three facts about what firefighters do when there is a fire, such as: acting fast, putting on uniforms, jumping into the truck, spraying water on the fire, and saving people.

Day 5 (page 88)

Answers describe how firefighters might feel when they wake up at night to the alarm and what they do to get ready. Answers should also include a picture.

Week 2

Day 1 (page 89)

1. B
2. C
3. A

Day 2 (page 90)

1. B
2. A
3. B

Day 3 (page 91)

1. C
2. A
3. Answers should describe what else Flynn and his family saw on their hike.

Day 4 (page 93)

1. B
2. A
3. C
4. Answers will vary. Example:

Beginning	Middle	End
Flynn and his family hike.	They meet a park ranger.	They hear about a wildfire and leave.

Day 5 (page 94)

Answers should describe what the park ranger says to the family and what they should do. Answers should include a picture.

Week 3

Day 1 (page 96)

1. A
2. C
3. B
4. Answers should describe which clues they found most useful in the poem and why.

Day 2 (page 97)

Answers should include underlined words or phrases about fire or fires from each text. Answers should also use three of the words or phrases in sentences.

Day 3 (page 98)

Effect (choose one): The fire made them warm; they sang songs; they made s'mores; they had a great night.

Effects (choose one): The ranger told the family; the fire burned a lot of trees; the ranger warned the family to leave.

Day 4 (page 99)

Answers should inlcude a completed poem about fire, using a student's own words and an illustration.

Day 5 (page 100)

Answers should include three clues about an object, the object's name, and a picture of the object.

Answer Key (cont.)

Unit 6

Week 1

Day 1 (page 101)

1. A
2. C
3. A

Day 2 (page 102)

1. B
2. C
3. B

Day 3 (page 103)

1. C
2. B
3. The problem is that the ball gets stuck in the baskets each time teams score. He could solve the problem by cutting holes in the baskets.

Day 4 (page 105)

1. B
2. C
3. A
4. Answers should include two changes made to the game, such as players dribbling the ball and a hoop replacing the peach basket.

Day 5 (page 106)

Answers should describe the student's favorite sports and tell how they could change it. Answers should also include a picture.

Week 2

Day 1 (page 107)

1. A
2. B
3. C

Day 2 (page 108)

1. C
2. B
3. C

Day 3 (page 109)

1. C
2. B
3. Answers may include that in a bounce pass, the ball bounces between players. It does not bounce in a chest pass.

Day 4 (page 111)

1. A
2. C
3. C
4. 1, 3, 2, 4

Day 5 (page 112)

Answers should describe a time when students helped someone or worked together with others. Answers should also include a picture.

Week 3

Day 1 (page 114)

1. B
2. A
3. C
4. Answers may include: wrapped, round, hard, roll, bounce, dribble, and throw.

Day 2 (page 115)

Answers should include basketball words from each text, such as *toss*, *basket*, *dribble*, and *ball*, and *point guard*, *dribble*, *ball*, *game*, *coach*, *score*, *court*, and *team*.

Day 3 (page 116)

"Passing Drills"—Characters: Zoe; the other kids at camp; Setting: basketball camp; Event: Answers will vary.

"Is It For Me?"—Characters: narrator; Setting: a room with a Christmas tree; under a Christmas tree; late at night; Event: Answers will vary.

Day 4 (page 117)

Answers should include diary entries as Zoe telling about her first day at basketball camp and how she feels. Answers should also include pictures.

Day 5 (page 118)

Answers should include words to complete a poem frame of "Is It for Me?" about a new present. Answers should also include a picture.

Unit 7

Week 1

Day 1 (page 119)

1. C
2. A
3. B

Day 2 (page 120)

1. C
2. B
3. A

Day 3 (page 121)

1. B
2. A
3. The main idea is that service dogs help people who use wheelchairs.

Day 4 (page 123)

1. C
2. B
3. C
4. Sample response:

1.	There is an earthquake.
2.	There is a big storm.
3.	A hiker is lost.

Day 5 (page 124)

Answers should describe what they would like a dog to help them do. Answers should also include pictures.

Answer Key (cont.)

Week 2

Day 1 (page 125)
1. B
2. C
3. A

Day 2 (page 126)
1. A
2. C
3. C

Day 3 (page 127)
1. B
2. C
3. Answers should include a prediction about what students think will happen to the peanut butter snacks.

Day 4 (page 129)
1. A
2. C
3. A
4. Answers should include three words or phrases describing Mac's award, such as giant, ribbons, and "Mac is our hero!"

Day 5 (page 130)
Answers should include a drawn and labeled award and writing about who it is for and why.

Week 3

Day 1 (page 132)
1. C
2. A
3. B
4. Answers should describe how they think the pup in the text might become a hero.

Day 2 (page 133)
Example

Questions	A New Student	Field Day Hero
Characters	Mac the dog	narrator, kids
One Key Detail	He is a service dog.	They put their ribbons together and give them to Mac.
Important Words About the Main Idea	school, Mac, dog, service, nuts, protect	field day, over, Mac, help, ribbons, award, hero

Day 3 (page 134)
Answers should include details about rescue dogs from both texts, such as having a great sense of smell, finding people who are trapped, being heroes, rescuing people, using smell to find people, and training.

Day 4 (page 135)
Answers should include illustrations and a sentence to end the story.

Day 5 (page 136)
Answers should include an article about Mac at the field day event and include a picture.

Unit 8

Week 1

Day 1 (page 137)
1. C
2. A
3. C

Day 2 (page 138)
1. C
2. A
3. B

Day 3 (page 139)
1. A
2. B
3. Answers should include that the author wants to inform/tell readers about what happens to the ocean during a hurricane.

Day 4 (page 141)
1. B
2. C
3. A
4. Answers may include: Strong winds can tear up trees; Rain can cause flooding; The ocean level may rise; Boats can get tossed by waves; The beach may get worn away.

Day 5 (page 142)
Answers should describe what students might see on a beach after a big storm. Answers should also include a picture.

Week 2

Day 1 (page 143)
1. A
2. A
3. B

Day 2 (page 144)
1. A
2. C
3. B

Day 3 (page 145)
1. C
2. B
3. Mark's family turns on flashlights and plays flashlight tag. They read scary books together.

Day 4 (page 147)
1. C
2. B
3. A
4. 2, 4, 1, 5, 3

Answer Key (cont.)

Day 5 (page 148)

Answers should include pictures of Mark before, during, and after the hurricane. Answer should also include a sentence describing how Mark's hurricane story ends.

Week 3

Day 1 (page 150)

1. A
2. C
3. C
4. Answers should describe how students would feel after listening to the weather report and why.

Day 2 (page 151)

Example

Questions	Time to Help	Radio Weather Report
What is the setting?	Mark's town and house; after the hurricane	a town where a hurricane hit; a radio station
What does the main character want?	Mark wants to help people; Mark wants to donate some clothes.	The radio host wants to tell people what is happening and wants people to call in.
What happens at the end?	Mark goes through his clothes to donate some.	The announcer asks people to call and tell how they are doing,

Day 3 (page 152)

Answers should include words or phrases from both texts that describe what happens during a hurricane, such as strong winds can tear up trees; rain can cause flooding; ocean levels may rise; boats can get tossed around; the beach may get worn away; and it is rainy and windy; lights start to flicker; it goes dark; the family plays flashlight tag.

Day 4 (page 153)

Answers should include a flyer for a donation event with an illustration. Students should include important details about the event.

Day 5 (page 154)

Answers should include responses to the imaginary dialogue with the radio host about the hurricane experience.

Unit 9

Week 1

Day 1 (page 155)

1. B
2. C
3. B

Day 2 (page 156)

1. B
2. B
3.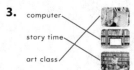

computer
story time
art class

Day 3 (page 157)

1. A
2. C
3. Answers could include that someone else can read, borrow, or look at the book.

Day 4 (page 159)

1. C
2. B
3. A
4. Answers should include three important facts about tiny libraries, such as they are small, they look like dollhouses, and people of all ages can take or trade books there.

Day 5 (page 160)

Answers should include the design and drawing of a tiny library and three rules for it.

Week 2

Day 1 (page 161)

1. B
2. A
3. B

Day 2 (page 162)

1. B
2. A
3. B

Day 3 (page 163)

1. A
2. C
3. Answers should include that she knows because she talks to them.

Day 4 (page 165)

1. A
2. C
3. B
4. 3, 2, 1, 4

Day 5 (page 166)

Answers should include a poster with important information about the club and a picture.

Answer Key (cont.)

Week 3

Day 1 (page 168)
1. C
2. A
3. B
4. Answers should describe where the text might be used and why, such as in front of a tiny library.

Day 2 (page 169)
Answers should include ways the book clubs are alike, such as books are members of the clubs, and ways that they are different, such as in one club the books learn to read.

Day 3 (page 170)
Answers should include such things as: Librarians are at the library; Many libraries have computers; Some libraries have story time; Some libraries have art classes.

Day 4 (page 171)
Answers should include a fictional story about what books might do after the library closes. Answers should also include a picture.

Day 5 (page 172)
Answers should include a note from the tiny library's perspective, telling people what the library wants people to know and including rules for its use.

Unit 10

Week 1

Day 1 (page 173)
1. C
2. B
3. A

Day 2 (page 174)
1. B
2. A
3. C

Day 3 (page 175)
1. A
2. C
3. Answers should include what students learned after reading the text.

Day 4 (page 177)
1. A
2. B
3. B
4. Answers might include: Pumpkins are ready to be picked in the fall; They turn from green to other colors; You can paint or carve them; You can eat them; They have seeds inside; You can bake the seeds and eat them.

Day 5 (page 178)
Answers should describe what students like to do with pumpkins. Answers should include pictures.

Week 2

Day 1 (page 179)
1. B
2. C
3. A

Day 2 (page 180)
1. C
2. B
3. A

Day 3 (page 181)
1. A
2. C
3. Answers should include that the pumpkin ghosts had gone when Harper came back with her camera.

Day 4 (page 183)
1. B
2. A
3. C
4. Example

Beginning	Middle	End
A pumpkin ghost shows up at Harper's house.	More pumpkins show up.	Harper gives the pumpkin ghosts some treats.

Day 5 (page 184)
Answers should describe what students saw as if they were Harper's friend, and it should include a picture.

Week 3

Day 1 (page 186)
1. C
2. A
3. B
4. Answers should describe what students would wear if they could have year-long costumes and why.

Day 2 (page 187)
Example

Questions	Apple Trees	Pumpkin Picking
When is the fruit picked?	Apples are picked in the fall.	Pumpkins are ready to be picked in the fall.
What colors might the fruit be?	Apples are red, pink, green, and yellow.	They turn from green to orange or other colors.
What can you do with the fruit?	Many people bake them into apple pies!	Carve, paint, and use them for decoration.

Answer Key (cont.)

Day 3 (page 188)

Answers should describe four similarities and two differences between the texts.

Day 4 (page 189)

Answers should include facts about a fruit of their choosing and include a picture. The fruit should be the story narrator.

Day 5 (page 190)

Answers should include dialogue for the boy and the mother in the text. Answers should include images to go with the dialogue.

Unit 11

Week 1

Day 1 (page 191)

1. B
2. A
3. A

Day 2 (page 192)

1. C
2. B
3. C

Day 3 (page 193)

1. C
2. B
3. Answers should include what students have learned about pirates after reading the text.

Day 4 (page 195)

1. C
2. B
3. C
4. Answers could include: She couldn't find work; She fought in a war dressed like a man; She got married; Her husband died; She sailed away; Her ship was attacked by pirates; She chose to stay and be a pirate; They were caught; She went to jail.

Day 5 (page 196)

Answers should describe a day in the life of a pirate and include a picture.

Week 2

Day 1 (page 197)

1. C
2. B
3. A

Day 2 (page 198)

1. B
2. C
3. A

Day 3 (page 199)

1. C
2. B
3. Cole's parents are in the park because they have planned a birthday surprise for him.

Day 4 (page 201)

1. C
2. A
3. B
4. 3, 1, 5, 2, 4

Day 5 (page 202)

Answers should include plans for a birthday surprise party, including who and how, and also include a picture.

Week 3

Day 1 (page 204)

1. B
2. A
3. B
4. Answers should describe how the pirate in the text is different from most pirates, especially in how this pirate does not like doing what other pirates do.

Day 2 (page 205)

Effect: They follow the treasure map.

Cause: Cole's parents tell him he can use the coins at the arcade.

Day 3 (page 206)

Example:

Questions	A Different Pirate	Dear Diary
Who is the main character or person?	Mary Read	a pirate
Do they want to be a pirate?	No, but she feels she must.	Not really. They say they are too honest for the job.

Day 4 (page 207)

A Pirate's Life For Me

Answers should include words to fill in the blanks in the song. Answers should also include a picture.

Day 5 (page 208)

Answers should include a diary entry from a pirate's perspective, telling what they want to do instead of being a pirate. A picture of the new job should be included.

Unit 12

Week 1

Day 1 (page 209)

1. A
2. B
3. C

Day 2 (page 210)

1. C
2. B
3. C

Answer Key (cont.)

Day 3 (page 211)

1. A
2. B
3. The cockroaches make noise by pushing air out of breathing holes in their bodies.

Day 4 (page 213)

1. B
2. B
3. A
4. Answers could include: Cockroaches can be kept in a dry fish tank with a lid; They need clean bedding; They need fresh water; They need food; They can eat dog food; They like apple slices.

Day 5 (page 214)

Answers should include writing as if students have a hissing cockroach for a pet, its name, where they got it, and how they care for it. The writing should include a picture that goes with the text.

Week 2

Day 1 (page 215)

1. C
2. A
3. A

Day 2 (page 216)

1. B
2. A
3. C

Day 3 (page 217)

1. A
2. A
3. The colorful plants attract more butterflies and bees.

Day 4 (page 219)

1. B
2. A
3. C
4. wings, bees, flowers, bugs

Day 5 (page 220)

Answers should include a design for a backyard garden, including the types of plants students would get, how they would decorate, and what they would do there. Student should draw pictures to go with the writing.

Week 3

Day 1 (page 222)

1. B
2. A
3. B
4. Answers should include how the letter changes student feelings about spiders in their house.

Day 2 (page 223)

Example

Questions	Catching Butterflies	Growing the Garden
How do they feel about butterflies?	The girl and her brother love butterflies.	They like to watch them and draw pictures of their beautiful wings.
What do they do with butterflies?	They try to catch them.	They watch, draw, and chase them.

Day 3 (page 224)

Answers should include four ways hissing cockroaches are different from the spiders in the poem.

Day 4 (page 225)

Answers should include three more reasons why the humans should be nice to the spiders. Answers should also include pictures.

Day 5 (page 226)

Answers should include a letter from a creature in nature written to the student. A picture should also be included.

Digital Resources

Accessing the Digital Resources

The digital resources can be downloaded by following these steps:

1. Go to **www.tcmpub.com/digital**

2. Use the 13-digit ISBN number to redeem the digital resources.

3. Respond to the question using the book.

4. Follow the prompts on the Content Clo ud website to sign in or create a new account.

5. The content redeemed will appear on your My Content screen. Click on the product to look through the digital resources. All file resources are available for download. Select files can be previewed, opened, and shared.

For questions and assistance with your ISBN redemption, please contact Shell Education.

email: customerservice@tcmpub.com

phone: 800-858-7339

Contents of the Digital Resources

- Standards Correlations
- Writing Rubric
- Fluency Rubric
- Class and Individual Analysis Sheets